Praise for *The Way of Forgiveness*

"In *The Way of Forgiveness,* Stephen Mitchell re-creates the biblical story of Joseph into a novelistic tale of self-discovery, tragedy, love, and reconciliation. He approaches this ageless act and respect, adding to it through his . His prose is rich with image psychological portraits of th storytelling, exceptionally we is a fine achievement." (starred review)

"*The Way of Forgiveness* is a beautiful retelling of one of the most profound and moving passages in the Bible. Stephen Mitchell has fashioned a deceptively simple version of the story of Joseph and his brothers, and given it back to the world in luminous prose. A unique and special kind of masterpiece."
—John Banville, winner of the Booker Prize for *The Sea*

"Stephen Mitchell is a tireless curator of wisdom whose life's work is nothing less than the study of human transformation. With *The Way of Forgiveness,* Mitchell has reached back in time to one of our oldest stories of grace and brought its lessons forward to us. The heart cannot help but be moved and healed by the treasure to be found in these pages."
—Elizabeth Gilbert, author of *Eat Pray Love*

"A rich and meaningful chronicle-cum-midrash."
—Cynthia Ozick, winner of the National Book Critics
Circle Award and of the PEN/Nabokov Award

"Evoking the ancient Jewish art of midrash, Mitchell has now novelized this timeless story, bringing to it a touch of metafiction, and a sometimes breezy and insouciant but always reverent style. Richly imagined and told in bite-size chapters, the book is compulsively readable and inspirational. It's a timeless tale retold in a timeless fashion." —*Booklist*

"Stephen Mitchell's vividly imagined narrative breathes interior life into the classic Joseph story, and offers the reader a generous and much needed gift—an incisive and moving account of the spiritual power of forgiveness."
—Elaine Pagels, author of *The Gnostic Gospels*

"A captivating contemporary retelling of the biblical story of Joseph." —*Publishers Weekly*

"How do you honestly and deeply 'interpret' a dream? By dreaming it onward. How do you honestly and deeply read a story from the Bible? By telling it onward, again and again, with a reverent imagination. Stephen Mitchell has beautifully reimagined the Biblical story of Joseph with an enhanced retelling in exquisite language and with subtle insight. You won't find a more moving, inspiring, and enlightening book on the Bible."
—Thomas Moore, author of *The Care of the Soul*

"With the gift of a storyteller and the knowledge of a Bible scholar, Mitchell engages in an extended work of midrash that breathes new life and meaning into familiar characters . . . . A pleasurable, enlightening, lively, and lyrical book."
—Jonathan Kirsch, *Jewish Journal*

"Stephen Mitchell retell[s] the biblical story of Jacob and his sons (and daughter), amplifying with a rich imagination the wellsprings of love and animus in their world. . . . However we read *The Way of*

Forgiveness—as another midrash on the biblical story of Jacob's sons or as the ethical will of a man in his eighth decade whose life and work have been inflected by nearly every culture that left some written record—the abiding message is one of 'love, compassion, and gratitude.'"   —Sidra DeKoven Ezrahi, *Tikkun*

"Not since *Joseph and the Amazing Technicolor Dreamcoat* has the tale of Joseph and his brothers sparkled as much as it does in Stephen Mitchell's fiction retelling of the story. With the voice of a Zen-trained narrator who's steeped in midrash, Mitchell weaves together the biblical text, insights about human psychology, and theological questions that refuse to settle for easy answers."   —*The Christian Century*

"A long, cool drink of understanding in a fractious and over-heated contemporary world of ill will and retribution."
                    —Bob Bahr, *Atlanta Jewish Times*

"Mitchell has . . . created a novel that will have you turning the pages to see what happens next or what gems of wisdom the author has discovered within a story we already know . . . . He has done a superb job . . . . In his approach to a story that has no surprises, he surprised me with the sensitivity and perception with which he retells the famous story. *The Way of Forgiveness* is a refreshing and thoughtful interpretation."
                    —Miriam Kates Lock, *Jerusalem Post*

"*The Way of Forgiveness* is a sparkling, joyous retelling of a story that seems endlessly opaque and hard to comprehend in the Bible. Stephen Mitchell has made the story wondrous, and a page-turner that takes us into a new, mysterious world, as palpable as the one we live in today."   —Paul Hawken, author of *Blessed Unrest*

Books by Stephen Mitchell

Poetry and Fiction

The Frog Prince • *Meetings with the Archangel* •
Parables and Portraits

Nonfiction

Joseph and the Way of Forgiveness • *A Mind at Home with
Itself* (with Byron Katie) • *A Thousand Names for Joy* (with
Byron Katie) • *Loving What Is* (with Byron Katie) •
The Gospel According to Jesus

Translations and Adaptations

Beowulf • *The Odyssey* • *The Iliad* • *Duino Elegies & The
Sonnets to Orpheus* • *The Second Book of the Tao* •
Gilgamesh • *Bhagavad Gita* • *Full Woman, Fleshly
Apple, Hot Moon: Selected Poems of Pablo Neruda* • *Genesis* •
*Ahead of All Parting: The Selected Poetry and Prose of Rainer
Maria Rilke* • *A Book of Psalms* • *The Selected
Poetry of Dan Pagis* • *Tao Te Ching* • *The Book of Job* •
The Selected Poetry of Yehuda Amichai (with Chana Bloch)

• *The Sonnets to Orpheus* • *The Lay of the Love and Death of Cornet Christoph Rilke* • *Letters to a Young Poet* • *The Notebooks of Malte Laurids Brigge* • *The Selected Poetry of Rainer Maria Rilke* • *Selected Poems of T. Carmi and Dan Pagis*

Edited by Stephen Mitchell

Question Your Thinking, Change the World: Quotations from Byron Katie • *The Essence of Wisdom* • *Bestiary: An Anthology of Poems about Animals* • *Song of Myself* • *Into the Garden: A Wedding Anthology* (with Robert Hass) • *The Enlightened Mind: An Anthology of Sacred Prose* • *The Enlightened Heart: An Anthology of Sacred Poetry* • *Dropping Ashes on the Buddha: The Teaching of Zen Master Seung Sahn*

For Children

The Ugly Duckling • *Iron Hans* • *Genies, Meanies, and Magic Rings* • *The Tinderbox* • *The Wishing Bone and Other Poems* • *The Nightingale* • *Jesus: What He Really Said and Did* • *The Creation*

The Way of Forgiveness

A STORY ABOUT LETTING GO

Stephen Mitchell

ST. MARTIN'S
ESSENTIALS
NEW YORK

First published as *Joseph and the Way of Forgiveness* in the United States by
St. Martin's Essentials, an imprint of St. Martin's Publishing Group

www.stmartins.com

Brief portions of this book are based on my translation, *Genesis*
(HarperCollins, 1996). One paragraph in the chapter "Learning Humility" first
appeared, in slightly different form, in *A Mind at Home with Itself* by Byron Katie
(HarperOne, 2017). In the description of Joseph's palace in the chapter "Life with
Asenath," I have pilfered some phrases from www.ancientegyptonline.co.uk
/malkatapalace.html. My version of the "Hymn to the Sun" in the chapter
"In-Laws" first appeared, in slightly different form, in *Bestiary: An Anthology of
Poems about Animals* (Frog, Ltd., 1996).

Lines from *The Collected Works of W. B. Yeats, Volume I: The Poems, Revised* by
W. B. Yeats, edited by Richard J. Finneran. Copyright © 1924 by The Macmillan
Company, renewed 1952 by Bertha Georgie Yeats. Reprinted with the permission
of Scribner, a division of Simon & Schuster, Inc. All rights reserved.

The Library of Congress Cataloging-in-Publication Data is available upon request

ISBN 978-1-250-23752-1 (hardcover)
ISBN 978-1-250-23753-8 (ebook)
ISBN 978-1-250-23989-1 (trade paperback)

Our books may be purchased in bulk for promotional, educational, or business
use. Please contact your local bookseller or the Macmillan Corporate and
Premium Sales Department at 1-800-221-7945, extension 5442, or by email at
MacmillanSpecialMarkets@macmillan.com.

First St. Martin's Essentials Paperback Edition: 2020

10 9 8 7 6 5 4 3 2 1

To Katie

Contents

⟡

Foreword

"JOSEPH AND HIS BROTHERS" is the final section of the Book of Genesis. Tolstoy called it the most beautiful story in the world. It takes its hero through a death and transformation, from the charming but arrogant brat of its first part to the master of reality of its last, and it has an all-embracing forgiveness at its core. Significantly, God doesn't appear in it. The storyteller's understanding of God was too clear to permit that. He knew that stories in which God appears can never be about God; they can only be about a *character* called "God." But "God" isn't God.

You may be wondering why I have reimagined "Joseph and His Brothers." Isn't it perfect as it is? Yes, certainly, whether you read it in the original Hebrew or in the more dignified, less earthy King James Version, and its beauty shines through even in the most vulgar or tone-deaf of modern translations. But, like most of Genesis, it's written in a style of extraordinary concision, so spare that it can compress pages of characterization into a single phrase. The storyteller leaves much of his tale hinted at but unstated, as if it were a hypertext with unprovided links. To take just the first example: "Jacob loved Joseph more than all his other children." This one phrase, which sets up the whole drama of the story—how tantalizing it is! Close, prolonged attention to it yields rich rewards. Many passages are like that: Japanese paper flowers, which unfurl when we place them in the water of the imagination.

That's why I was so attracted to this story: not just because of what it says, but because of what it leaves unsaid. It cries out for the ancient Jewish art of midrash, or creative transformation—a way of inhabiting the text in order to deepen your understanding of it. To penetrate into these unsaid realms, you need a certain degree of irreverence—or, more accurately, reverence masking as irreverence. Conventional reverence means standing at a distance from the text so that the light is refracted through it, as through a stained-glass window. With midrash, you need to get much closer than that. You need to swallow the text whole, digest it, assimilate it, excrete it, walk around with it resonating inside you for hours or days, let it become your constant meditation and your unceasing prayer.

Joseph is the most spiritually mature character in the Hebrew Bible, someone who has literally ascended from the depths to a freedom that every reader can recognize and enjoy. But how does he get there? How does he learn a deeper humanity, sitting at the feet of his own suffering, and move from the dreamer of visionary dreams to the dream interpreter, the shaman of the tribe? What allows him to grow beyond anger and resentment at his brothers' murderous jealousy? The forgiveness he embodies at the end of the story is unparalleled elsewhere in the Bible, even in the Gospels, where Jesus tells us to forgive seventy times seven but doesn't show us what forgiveness looks like. (That wasn't his job.) In the Joseph story we can see the enlightened mind in action, the mind in harmony with the way things are, after the deadly tricks of the ego have been met with understanding. Joseph realizes that there is a vast, compassionate intelligence always at work beneath the surface of the apparent. He has come to the point where, with

> all hatred driven hence,
> The soul recovers radical innocence
> And learns at last that it is self-delighting,
> Self-appeasing, self-affrighting,
> And that its own sweet will is Heaven's will.

I wanted to provide you not only with the what of his transformation, but also with the how. To that purpose, I have enlisted the help of a team of imaginary second-century Galilean rabbis. (Sometimes the only way to tell the truth is to make it up.)

I should also warn you that the Egypt of this book is an imaginary country, in which anachronisms may sneak up and tap you on the shoulder. The dream systems and textbooks, the three schools of divination, the *haute cuisine* with its mustard/white-wine sauce—I imagined them all, for my own pleasure and, I hope, for yours.

◇

Prologue

BEFORE I BEGIN THIS MIDRASH, I need to go back a genera-
tion and remind you of how Joseph was born—with what
longing and exultation. I might have begun with Abraham,
his great-grandfather, the first Jewish ancestor, who heard a
voice without words and followed it into the future like a
man walking blindfolded through thick forest, moonless
night; or with Joseph's grandfather Isaac, that damaged soul,
who never got past the moment of dread when he lay trussed
up on the altar, a carving knife quivering against his breast,
his father's huge eyes above him, exalted and horrible; or with
Jacob, his father, who cheated his twin, Esau, out of the
Blessing, fled from Canaan to Mesopotamia, and prospered
there by somewhat dubious means. But those are stories for
another occasion. Here I will tell you only the prelude to Joseph's birth.

As soon as Jacob arrived on the outskirts of Haran in Mesopotamia, he fell in love with his beautiful cousin Rachel. For
seven years he served Laban, her father, in return for her, and

the seven years seemed to him just a few days, so deeply did
he love her. But Laban cheated him; he substituted his elder
daughter, Leah, in the shimmering darkness of the wedding
tent, and Jacob made love to her all night long, and when dawn
came, he was devastated, furious, heartsick at having given the
first of himself, the best of himself, to the wrong woman, and
he ran to his father-in-law's tent in protest. But he gained Rachel only by agreeing to serve Laban for seven more years. He
was a polygamist by necessity, like his grandfather Abraham—
not by choice, like his descendants David and Solomon.
(Thus, the strict Biblical definition of marriage is "the union
of one man with one woman or more.")

Leah, the unloved wife, turned out to be unfailingly fruitful: for four years, every spring, as the meadows grew rich with
wildflowers, she would give birth to a healthy boy. But Rachel couldn't conceive. Her lovemaking with Jacob came to
seem like a mockery, her womb an emptiness and a desolation.
After four years of constant failure, she cried out to Jacob,
"Give me children, or I will die," and demanded that he sleep
with her handmaid, "so that I too may have children, through
her." Jacob couldn't bear to refuse his beloved anything she
asked for, and the slave gave birth to two sons in two years.
(In the meantime, Leah had stopped bearing children.
"Enough!" Rachel had said to Jacob. "My sister has four boys
already. No more visits to her tent!") Then Leah insisted that
he sleep with *her* handmaid, who also gave birth to two sons.
Later, as a result of some sisterly dealmaking, Leah bore him
two more sons and a daughter, Dinah, who makes a brief, sad
appearance in our story. Finally—finally, after fifteen years of
misery and supplication—Rachel conceived. She named the

boy Joseph, which means He Has Taken Away (that is, God
Has Taken Away My Humiliation).

Joseph was by far the most beautiful of all the twelve
children. From the very beginning, Jacob and Rachel adored
him.

Six years later, Rachel died giving birth to a second child.
During her last conscious moments, she named him Ben-ōni
(Son of My Misfortune). As dearly as Jacob wished to honor
his beloved's choice, this name was beyond what he could en-
dure. So he renamed the child Benjamin (Son of the Right
Hand).

When Rachel died, Jacob felt as if he had died with her.

I.
The Favorite Son

Why Jacob Loved Joseph Best

JACOB LOVED JOSEPH FAR MORE than his other children. This partiality was obvious to everyone, especially to the other sons. It could be considered Jacob's tragic flaw, if our story weren't a comedy—that is, if it didn't have a happy ending.

Jacob loved him because Joseph was the child of Rachel, the beloved. The boy looked just like his mother, except that his beauty was male, like a melody transposed into another key. His large dark-brown eyes sparkled with intelligence and mischief, as hers once had. He smiled with the same full, elegantly curved lips. He laughed the way she used to laugh. (When Jacob said something that greatly amused her, laughter would take over her whole body; she would rock back and forth with it; tears would pour down her cheeks.) Everything about the boy reminded Jacob of her. Joseph was her memorial, her incarnation, the only remnant of her left in the physical world.

Yes, there was Benjamin, but he didn't resemble her as closely. Besides, despite Jacob's many heartfelt prayers not to, he still resented the boy for causing her death.

Hebron

JACOB LIVED IN THE HEBRON VALLEY, surrounded by the Judean Mountains, three thousand feet above sea level and twenty miles southwest of Jerusalem, which even then, almost thirty-seven hundred years ago, was a city unfathomably ancient. Hebron is where Abraham had entertained angels unawares, near the great oaks of Mamre. The three unearthly visitors had arrived from nowhere, looking like men, and only after they had finished the meal had Abraham noticed their luminescence.

Since Jacob's livelihood depended on his flocks and herds, he and his remaining wife, Leah, with the two concubines, the thirteen children, and the wives of the married sons, would pitch their tents in one spot for a while and then move on. He was a rich man, rich enough so that years before, on his journey back from Mesopotamia, he had been able to make his brother, Esau (not out of brotherly love, but out of terror and residual guilt), the gift of two hundred twenty sheep, two hundred twenty goats, thirty milch camels with their calves, forty cows, ten bulls, and thirty donkeys—a gift he could easily afford.

If we were to visit the camp, you and I, we might find Jacob sitting before his tent in the cool of the day. As soon as he saw strangers approaching, he would, in his great courtesy, run out to meet us, unconcerned with his patriarchal dignity, which required movement at a slow and stately pace. He would bring water for us to wash our feet, and he would invite us to stretch out under one of the oak trees while he prepared dinner. Then he would slaughter a calf or a lamb and have it roasted, tell the women to bake bread, and serve us the meat and bread, along with a generous supply of milk and yogurt, and we would sit and eat and talk and laugh in good fellowship under the oak tree, as he sat with us, taking pleasure in our pleasure.

But it's better not to disturb him. So let us go as invisible presences. Come. I'll guide you.

Jacob has camped in one of the lush valleys around the city. It is a warm day in springtime. The grass is thick. The hills are red and yellow with poppies and mustard flowers. You can see flocks and herds everywhere, in the valley or on the slopes, grazing or lying in the shadow of the oak trees, accompanied by a few men and boys carrying slingshots and shepherd's crooks and clothed in tan-colored woolen robes fastened at the waist by broad leather belts. As we approach them, you can smell the fat odor of sheep and the more pungent odor of the goats. Look, there's Benjamin, nine years old, sitting on a log and playing a reed pipe, repeating the same tune over and over. The shrubs on the hill to our right are mastic, myrtle, kermes oak, and buckthorn, which the goats love. There are other varieties of oak here in the valley, some of them with ancient, gnarled trunks, along with cedars and almond trees. Over there, three cypresses point to the sky. Behind them is an olive grove, whose leaves the wind blows green and gray.

Now we're coming to the tents. This large one in front is Jacob's, where Joseph sleeps. Surrounding it, in a ragged half circle, are Leah's tent, the tents of the ten grown-up sons, the tent of Dinah, Jacob's only daughter, and the tents of the concubines, Bilhah and Zilpah, who are sitting outside now, chatting and carding wool. They are in their mid-thirties, Bilhah still thin and placid, Zilpah almost as energetic as in the days when, at Leah's insistence, Jacob slept with her and was astounded at the girl's sexual boldness. Young children, the boys and girls of the older sons, run around them barefoot or play in the shadows of the trees.

The sun is low. Soon it will be time to retire for the evening. Some of the brothers are pasturing their flocks in meadows a day's journey away; they won't come home tonight. Most are nearby, and if we stay, we will see them walking back to their wives and children.

Where is Joseph? He is in Jacob's tent, stretched out on two embroidered pillows, waiting for his father to return.

In Jacob's Tent

AFTER RACHEL DIED, JOSEPH BECAME Jacob's talisman and his almost exclusive focus. Joseph softened the old man's grief with his brilliance, charm, and constant good humor. Jacob could hardly bear to be without him; when he was by himself, he often felt overwhelmed by despair. So he kept Joseph close during the day, and at night he granted him the privilege of sleeping beside him. Joseph was the only child who spent the evenings with his father.

Jacob felt his heart ease a bit in the boy's presence. He loved to tell him the ancient stories, and Joseph loved to listen: about the Garden of Delight, where Yahweh* walked in the cool of the day and where he planted two trees, the Tree of Life first and then the Tree of the Knowledge of Good and Evil, which he compassionately forbade to Adam, and the talking serpent tempted Eve, and she was beguiled and ate, and Adam too was

---

* יהוה (Yahweh) is a name for the "God" character, often translated into English as "the Lord."

beguiled, and he too ate, for love of her, and they were ban-
ished from the Garden, and only when we eat of the fruit of
the Tree of Wisdom, which is the Tree of Life, can we return
to our original innocence; about Abel and his elder brother,
Cain, who thought he had lost everything when Yahweh rejected his offering, and he turned his anger against his brother
and slew him, and when Yahweh asked where Abel was, he
said, "Am I my brother's keeper?"; about Lamech, who married two women, Adah and Zillah, and Adah gave birth to
Jabal, the ancestor of those who live in tents, and to Jubal, the
ancestor of those who play the lyre and the flute, while Zillah
gave birth to Tubal, the ancestor of those who forge copper
and iron tools; about the sons of God, who came down to
earth, and when they saw how beautiful were the daughters
of men, they had sex with as many of them as they wanted,
and of their embraces were the giants born; about the call to
Noah, and the ark, and the animals, two by two, and the great
flood, and the rainbow's promise, and the time Noah got drunk
in his tent, and Ham went in and cut off his father's genitals;
about Nimrod, whom the Gentiles call Gilgamesh, a king
powerful beyond all others, violent, splendid, who strutted
through the great city of Uruk, trampling its citizens like a
wild bull; about the Tower of Babel, which the stupid Baby-
lonians built because they wanted to reach the heavens, in the
days when the whole earth was one language. After his father's
voice had grown silent in the darkness, Joseph would turn the
stories over in his mind as he waited for sleep to carry him off
into other realms.

But it was especially about Abraham that Jacob loved to
speak—his esteemed grandfather, whom he had never met.

Joseph would listen with awe, wide-eyed, to the stories of that great man, who heard God speak to him in the vast stillness of his mind. It was not a voice from the outside. The voice had no words at first. Abraham listened to it with all his attention, and eventually he bowed his head to what the voice was telling him, excruciatingly difficult though it was. The voice was telling him to leave everything behind, everything he loved most: mother and father, home and country, his beloved wife, the children he had not yet begotten, his own life—even his own life. If you love God, Jacob said, you must be ready to lose everything, gratefully, as Abraham had understood. "And you too will understand someday," Jacob would say to the boy, with tears in his eyes.

Being Beautiful

JOSEPH HAD BEEN SPOILED FROM the beginning, not by his parents' adoration (there can never be too much of a good thing), but by their lack of discernment. There is an aura around those who are physically beautiful, and when beauty is combined with extraordinary intelligence, it seems as if some kind of divine being has descended to earth, who can do no wrong and whose every whim cries out to be indulged. From an early age Joseph realized his effect on his parents. He acted toward them with the benevolent condescension that a great lord shows to his faithful retainers.

By the time he was thirteen, his beauty was on the tongues of women in the villages for miles around; they would jostle at the market to catch a glimpse of him. In addition to Hebrew, he spoke three languages fluently, and he had mastered the sciences of geometry, astronomy, and accounting. His father depended on him in all business matters, never bothering to consult his other sons.

Joseph treated his brothers with an easy neglect. All his life it had been obvious that he was the chosen one. He had nothing against the sons of Leah and the concubines' sons; they were decent men, in their own crude, ignorant way. But they were clearly inferiors, supporting players in the high drama that he knew would be his own life. Their dull eyes were like the dull eyes of their mothers—sheep eyes, goat eyes—and their sensibilities, adequate enough for shepherds, were unfit to keep up with a superior intelligence like his. He was friendly, and as respectful as he could manage to be, but he looked through them. He walked across the surface of their attention without pausing, like someone on his way to an important meeting, who has no time to linger.

❖

Favorites

YAHWEH FAVORS ABEL OVER CAIN, Sarah favors Isaac over Ishmael, Isaac favors Esau while Rebecca favors Jacob, Jacob favors Joseph over all his other sons. What's wrong with this picture? Furthermore, does congenital favoritism belong only to the archetypal Jewish family, or is it simply the way of the world?

There's a big difference, of course, between *having* favorites and *playing* favorites. I'm not very interested in a world without preferences. Even a buddha, when asked if she'd like vanilla or chocolate for her ice-cream cone, might say vanilla, though on a different day she might give a different answer. "The Great Way* isn't difficult," says an old Zen poem, "for those who are unattached to their preferences." Some of us can't help feeling more affinity with one child than with an-

---

* "The Great Way" means a life in perfect harmony with the Tao (reality: the way things are).

other, but we *can* help turning that affinity into preferential treatment. We can, and we do.

Jacob, though, didn't. He couldn't. He could never find a way to be a good father to his twelve other children. He himself had grown up without a father's love, in a state of constant craving for Isaac's approval, until the craving led him, under his mother's influence, to fraud, theft, and a guilt that lasted for decades. He had never learned impartiality; his parents' favoritism had seeped into the very organs of his perception. Moreover, Leah had been forced on him by his cheating father-in-law, and though he was kind to her, he had never loved her. Her children and the handmaids' children didn't feel like his, because their mothers weren't Rachel, the true wife. And though he did his best to love them, there was little warmth in it.

Can you see how this will play out? It has to play out, since there is nothing hidden that won't eventually be revealed. Whatever blind spots we refuse to acknowledge will burst into external reality at some point, to be seen, to be heard, to be either suffered or understood. Thus, in the closed system of the family, the momentum of Jacob's favoritism was conserved in all interactions, through all collisions and separations. It transformed itself into arrogance and entitlement in Joseph, and in the brothers into a toxic resentment.

The Ten Brothers

BEFORE WE PROCEED ANY FURTHER, let's move our focus to these ten half-brothers. Who were they? What were they like?

All ten of them were rough fellows, more like their mothers than their father, without any of Jacob's high-strung sensibilities or responsiveness to the demands of the spirit. They were bred to be shepherds, and they were content with no more than that. There was a particularly strong bond among (or between) the full brothers, but as Joseph grew up, all ten felt the bond that arises from having a common enemy.

Reuben was the tallest and strongest of them. As the first-born, he was the bearer of his father's Blessing, until a troubling incident that you'll hear about in the next chapter. Because of this transgression, Reuben had been demoted from the rank of firstborn, and the Blessing had been given to Judah instead.

Simeon and Levi looked like twins, though they had been born a year apart. If anyone needed to learn gentleness from the sheep they tended, it was these two. They were brutal, stupid, and irascible, and their violence had once gotten the whole family into trouble. Here's how it happened:

One day Dinah went to the Hivite city of Shechem, unchaperoned, to visit some girlfriends of hers. She was in a flirty mood, and when she met Shechem, son of the king of the city, she found him irresistible. He felt the same way about her. There was an immediate intimacy between them, and, young and hot-blooded as they were, they saw no reason to hold back from each other in any way. So they slept together. That night, they exchanged vows of eternal love and promised to seal that love in public, in the presence of their families. In the morning, the young man begged his father to make formal arrangements for the marriage. So Hamor went out to Jacob's camp with a few senior officials. He offered Jacob a very high brideprice, along with concessions that any father should have been thrilled with. Jacob nodded his head but didn't commit himself; he sensed the young man's urgency through the extravagance of the offering, and he knew he could hold out for an even better deal. He told Hamor that he would give the request his serious consideration and would speak about it with the girl's mother, who of course had to be consulted.

When Simeon and Levi heard what had happened, they were incensed. It was beneath the dignity of a daughter of Jacob to consort with a Canaanite, they thought, even if he was a prince; and anyway, he must have taken advantage of her innocence—to be blunt, he must have raped her. So they accosted the young man outside the city walls and beat him up rather badly. Jacob had to exert all his diplomatic skill, along with lavish gifts and a good measure of groveling, to propitiate Hamor. Of course, Hamor said, there was no question of marriage into such a family of thugs. (Dinah, forbidden the young man's company, was heartbroken. She never married.)

In later years, the story swelled to grotesque proportions in the two brothers' telling, and when they were in their cups, they would even boast of tricking the whole male population of the city into circumcising themselves, and then, on the third day, when the Hivite men were still in pain, of "rescuing" Dinah, murdering all the men, stealing their livestock, and enslaving their widows and children. None of Simeon and Levi's drinking companions took them seriously when they launched into their tale of the massacre, since they were known to be outrageous liars, even when sober. There was also the fact that the city of Shechem was still a bustling metropolis, inhabited by Hivite women and children and by Hivite men with mercifully uncircumcised penises between their legs.

So much for Leah's second and third sons.

Judah, the fourth son, was reputed to be as fierce as a lion's cub, and that is true, on the rare occasions when his temper was aroused. But he was also the most mature of the ten half-brothers. You'll hear more about him later, and about the fateful encounter with his daughter-in-law, Tamar.

As for the sons of the handmaids (Dan, Naphtali, Gad, and Asher) and Leah's youngest sons (Issachar and Zebulun, who was affectionately called Zeb), they figure in our story mostly as a background grumble: the Jewish equivalent of a Greek chorus.

Tattletale

FROM TIME TO TIME JACOB instructed Joseph to report on his ten half-brothers. Joseph enjoyed the job; he felt like one of God's recording angels. When he told on them, it wasn't out of malice. He was always frank with his father. He had no sense of discretion, and he gave no thought to the consequences his brothers might face from these reports. It never even occurred to him to put himself in their place.

In contrast to his brothers, he was usually free to come and go as he wished. Sometimes he served as assistant to Bilhah's and Zilpah's four sons, who put up with the boy's chatter and even let themselves be charmed by his flights of fancy. After he tattled on them, though, they knew better than to let their guard down again.

What could the men have been doing? Slacking off on the job? But isn't "slacking off" the *definition* of being a shepherd? "A god has given us this leisure," as Virgil's shepherd Tityrus sings. You keep one eye on the flock, and for the rest, you idle your time away, singing love songs to your raven-haired,

cherry-lipped, almond-eyed, amorous shepherdess sweetheart
or improvising on your flute or harp, a spiritual descendant of
Jubal (or is it Jabal?). In the fifth-century *Midrash on Genesis*,
two of our rabbis, convinced that the virtuous Joseph was obligated to report the brothers' misdemeanors, guessed at something more nefarious. Rabbi Meïr said, "The brothers must
have been eating limbs from living animals"—one of the hei-
nous sins that automatically excluded someone from the rab-
binic heaven. Rabbi Shimon, on the other hand, said, "They
were having sex with Canaanite girls." He was right.

One fine day, Joseph wandered out to a distant meadow
where he thought the four men might be. As he descended
from the top of a knoll, he saw Asher behind a clump of bushes,
naked, with a naked Kenite girl in his arms. (Joseph recognized her; she lived in a nearby village.) Asher was feeding her
from a bunch of grapes, in a moment of obviously postcoital
intimacy. As soon as the girl saw Joseph, she screamed and
covered herself. Asher, looking sheepish, said, "We're just having our fun. Please don't tell Father." Joseph snorted, turned
on his heels, and walked home. He had learned a contempt
for sexual promiscuity from his monogamous-at-heart father.
When Jacob heard of the incident, he called all four men to
his tent and berated them. Bilhah and Zilpah looked on in
shame.

Four months later, Joseph happened on Naphtali in fla-
grante delicto behind a bush in a different meadow, with a
girl from a different Kenite village.

He also brought his father several reports of Simeon and
Levi getting drunk and brawling with the men of neighboring towns.

But the most serious instance of his talebearing concerned big Reuben, the firstborn. One afternoon when Joseph was fourteen—it was a mild March day; the meadows were ablaze with poppies, anemones, mustard, iris, lupine—he was walking past the women's tents when he heard the sound of moaning from the tent of Bilhah, his dead mother's slave. He hesitated, but then he couldn't help coming closer and peeping in through the tent's front flap. Bilhah was lying there, naked, in Reuben's embrace. Joseph gasped. It was as if Reuben had taken his father's dignity and smeared it with feces. How could he have dared to do such a thing? Bilhah was his father's concubine; it was, symbolically, like sleeping with his own mother. Had he forced her? Had she given her consent? Both options were unthinkable. Joseph ran to Jacob's tent frightened, enraged, weeping with shame for his father, compelled to report what he had just, horribly, seen.

In the Greater Scheme of Things

"THE WORDS OF A TALEBEARER are like wounds," says the Book of Proverbs.

The brothers were deeply offended by Joseph's tattling. They resented him not only as their father's darling, but also as his spy. Joseph's very presence made them feel uncomfortable. It felt like a judgment, an attack. When they saw him approaching on his nasty little missions, they hardened their hearts and drew back into themselves. Their usual mode of speech to him was sarcasm, though when their father was present they mustered enough self-control to act with civility. Joseph, for his part, was oblivious of his brothers' resentment. He interpreted their sarcasm as churlishness and ill-temper, and he couldn't imagine that it had anything to do with him.

At what point does innocence turn into willful blindness, trust into naïveté, appropriate self-esteem into narcissism? But if Joseph hadn't been so obtuse, he would never have been able to arouse his brothers' hatred, and thus he would never be sold into Egypt, and thus the whole family would die of starvation in the coming famine. So in the greater scheme of things, his failure of empathy was everyone's salvation. And his moral flaws—the arrogance and insensitivity that resulted in such apparent mistakes as talebearing and flaunting his father's preference—were really blessings, woven into a deeper texture of reality. The very notion of mistakes is questionable here; later on, our storyteller shows that he sees it as self-centered short-term thinking. What seems to be a mistake in our lives may actually be a step forward that leads to the Great Way, though we had no way of recognizing that at the time.

The Coat of Many Colors

WHEN JOSEPH WAS SEVENTEEN, his father bought him a coat of many colors. It was the pièce de résistance of a Midianite caravan headed southwest. Jacob spent a whole morning bargaining for it, and in the end, he had to pay through the nose, so brightly had desire glittered from his eyes. The coat had been woven of the finest wool, dyed scarlet, crimson, maroon, yellow, green, royal blue, turquoise, and Tyrian purple. Its collar and the ends of its sleeves were threaded with gold and silver, and on its front was embroidered a scene of the earthly paradise: at the top shone the sun, moon, and stars, and underneath them was a garden of brilliant flowers, in the middle of which, on either side of the Tree of Life, two curlicue-bearded angels, with large furled eagle's wings, stood facing each other. Both were grinning, as if Yahweh had just told them an excellent joke.

What had Jacob been thinking when he bought this coat? Certainly not about the consequences, and in that blindness he resembled his favorite son. He saw only what he wanted to

see: an occasion for lavishing his affection on Joseph by ex-
pressing it in the most material of ways, like a rich man who
buys a diamond ring for his young mistress while skimping
with his wife and children. There was a desperate, an almost
demented quality to his passion for Joseph; you might even say
that it was a form of idol worship. But the genius of the un-
conscious mind, which functions as a mode of providence, was
clearly at work here. It is Jacob's very unwisdom that forces the
plot of our story to its tipping point. In the words of Job:

> My worst fears have happened;
>> my nightmares have come to life.

What Jacob most feared was losing Joseph. But that loss was
precisely what his gift precipitated.

After his purchase, Jacob held a ceremony to mark the occasion. He killed the fatted calf and told everyone to eat and
be merry. During the feast, he presented the coat to Joseph and
held it as the young man put his arms through its sleeves. "You
are the true son," he whispered in Joseph's ear, with love and
sorrow. "You are the true son of the true wife."

Later that day, Joseph told his brothers what their father
had whispered to him.

Levi gave voice to what they all were feeling. "The true son?
The true wife?" he snarled. "Does that make us bastards? Does
it make our mothers whores?"

Levi is always so irritable, Joseph thought.

On Edge

JOSEPH PARADED AROUND IN the coat every day. It was gorgeous in itself, but it was also a visible sign of his chosenness, and it set the brothers' teeth on edge. They began to call him "the little prick" behind his back, and sometimes to his face.

Their hatred grew by the day.

The First Dream

ONE NIGHT, AT THE BEGINNING of the spring harvest, Joseph had a dream: he and his brothers were out in a field binding barley sheaves, and suddenly his sheaf stood up, and their sheaves formed a ring around it and bowed down to it in allegiance.

As soon as he woke up, he knew that the dream was of the utmost importance.* He could have kept it to himself and mused on it, instead of blurting it out to his brothers, but because he projected his own delight onto them, he didn't hesitate to let them know. It was a true dream, after all; that is, it was a dream that would someday come true, a dream of salvation, and it just so happened that he was at the center of it. (It was only right, of course, that he should be at the center.) What they needed to be saved from, he didn't bother to ask.

---

* Rabbi Yehuda ben Eleazar of Safed said, "Joseph could distinguish between an ordinary dream and a numinous dream. As it is said, 'In a dream, in a vision of the night, / when deep sleep falls upon men, / God opens their inner ears / and seals their minds with instruction.'" (Job 33:15–16)

The point was the salvation, which was for them all, the whole family. His brothers would be as thrilled as he was!

Early that morning, before they all went out with the flocks and herds, Joseph sent word that they should meet him behind his father's tent. The sun had risen, the birds were singing, and though there was still a nip in the air, the day was going to be a warm one. When they had all arrived (Issachar was the last to straggle in, yawning), Joseph told them he had dreamed a marvelous dream. He laughed as he described it to them, and when he was finished, he looked as if he expected them to clap their hands and rejoice with him.

The brothers were shocked. Then their shock turned into dismay, their dismay into a dull rage. *Unbelievable,* they thought, *the brazenness of this arrogant little shit as he rubs his superiority in our faces.*

"So you're supposed to rule over us?" Simeon sneered. "Is that what your dream means?"

What's the matter with him? Joseph thought. *This dream is very good news.*

Later

THE BROTHERS MET. They were buzzing with rage, like hornets in a poked nest. Words spilled out.

"It can't go on like this."

"We've got to *do* something."

"What? What can we do?"

"He's lying. He didn't dream any such thing."

"But what if it's true? That's even worse."

"It would all be perfect without him."

"It would be better if he had never been born."

Eyes darted to other eyes, then to the ground. *It would be better if he were dead,* they were all thinking.

The Second Dream

THREE NIGHTS LATER, Joseph had a second dream. The dream was so vivid that he felt as if it were taking place before his waking eyes. *I am dreaming,* he said to himself in the dream. But whose voice was this? The self who heard the words or the self who spoke them? Were they the same? Did he even have a body now?

His consciousness seemed to be floating, expanding on all sides, alert for some event that was on the cusp of becoming. He was looking up at the sky—was it day or night?—and now he was *in* the sky, and now he *was* the sky. A luminous figure glided into sight. It was the sun, but it had the form of a man, and it was also his father. Then in glided a woman who was also the moon, and it was his mother, alive again. Then eleven smaller figures, his brothers: eleven flickering stars. They all bowed to the ground (suddenly there was a ground) before him. It was the most matter-of-fact gesture imaginable, a simple acknowledgment. They were stating what had been obvious to him all his life. Everyone knew it; they just hadn't known that they knew. *This is a dream,* he said to himself, *but it is true.*

He opened his eyes. He remembered everything. It was a second dream of salvation, even more powerfully shown than the first one. He could hardly believe his good fortune—*their* good fortune, since it affected the whole family. His father was part of it too, this time, and so was his mother. What did it mean that she had bowed in front of him, even though she was dead? How could that be a portent of the future? But it didn't matter. This was obviously a second dream of the utmost importance.

He lay there for a few minutes, savoring its power and the warmth of his body under the blanket. Then he stood up, washed, dressed, and hurried out of the tent. He had to tell his brothers. Surely this time they would recognize what a blessing had been granted to them, through him. The meaning couldn't be clearer. How happy they would be!

He was still smiling, though he wasn't aware of it. The smile clung to his lips for a moment, like a dewdrop on the tip of a blade of grass.

Not Happy

THE BROTHERS WERE NOT HAPPY.

Nor was Jacob, when Joseph told him. Jacob scolded him and commanded him not to tell them about any future dreams. The act of bowing down before his own son was humiliating, and it was obvious how much ill will it would cause among his other sons. But Jacob kept thinking about this dream for a long time afterward.

The boy was extraordinary in many ways, and heart-achingly beautiful. His intelligence, too, was beyond anything Jacob had ever encountered, and he was quick-witted as well, eloquent, practical, and charming. There had never been a reason to worry about his future. But after this dream, Jacob began to worry. Sometimes he was so alarmed by his thoughts that he couldn't fall asleep. He would watch Joseph's sleeping figure and listen to his breathing, and images of great peril would rise in him, quickening the pace of his heartbeat. Many times he prayed for Joseph's safety, but his prayers stayed earth-bound, like birds that have lost their wings.

What did the dream of subordination mean? He knew God's disregard for conventional order, but this would be going too far. It was one thing for the younger brother to be favored over the elder, but for the father to bow down before his son? That would be unheard of, intolerable. Surely the dream couldn't mean that.

But if not that, what *did* it mean? He worried about Joseph's self-confidence. It is dangerous to think so highly of yourself. On the other hand, the boy was lavishly blessed, and only a fool would fail to recognize that degree of blessing in himself. No, he would be fine, whatever happened. He was destined for great things, however God in His mysterious grace decided to bring them to pass. Jacob was sure of that. But then he had been sure that his beloved Rachel would always be at his side.

Still, it would all turn out for the best. He knew it would. He hoped it would.

The Last Straw

AH, BUT HOPE ISN'T ENOUGH. It's the Siamese twin of fear. It's the projection of a small personal desire onto the infinite possibilities of the future.

We have come to a point where our story's world has become fatally unstable. Think of it as a balance scale. Up to now, with Joseph in one weighing pan and his ten half-brothers in the other pan, there has been an equilibrium of sorts. But now our storyteller is about to put an additional weight into one of the pans, and the pointer will tip all the way over to one side. Which pan is rising, which sinking? There's no way to tell yet. All we can know is that the center will not hold.

And the weight that's about to drop: what specifically is it? Joseph's second dream? Some undisclosed thoughtlessness on his part? Or will that roughneck Simeon simply wake up one arbitrary morning in a foul mood, so that the mere sight of his beautiful brother, the chosen one, the delight of his father's soul, is enough to tip him over into a murderous rage? Can we know? Do we care?

I am reminded of the old Arabian story about the greedy camel driver who piles bale after bale of straw onto his favorite animal. Finally, eager to squeeze out one last bit of profit, he places still another wisp of straw on top of the load, and the camel's back breaks. A foolish friend of his comes to visit, in an effort to help him assess the situation and avoid future disasters. The friend examines the dead camel and the bales of straw scattered over the ground; then, in an effort to isolate the cause, he asks the camel driver to show him which straw was the last one. The driver chases him out of the yard with a measuring rod.

Murder

THE BROTHERS HAD HEARD the story of Cain and Abel from Jacob's lips, but it meant nothing to them. Like all the old stories, it had happened beyond resonance, in a distant past that had nothing to do with their present. They didn't realize that the first murder was a direct consequence of the first jealousy and that Cain's jealousy was theirs as well. Cain's jealousy, like theirs, resulted from a sense of rejection. He had brought a handsome offering of fruits and vegetables to the altar, in good faith, but Yahweh rejected it, and Cain "was very troubled, and his face fell." (Of *course* his face fell!) About this verse, an ancient Galilean rabbi, Hanina the Shoemaker, said, "He was like a child who, after he is punished, takes it out on his smaller brother. As it is said, 'Happy shall he be who dashes your little ones against the rocks.'" (Ps. 137:9) Another ancient rabbi, Shimon bar Zonin of Magdala, said, "Cain thought that if his brother died, the Lord would love him best. As it is said, 'He will swallow up death in victory.'" (Isa. 25:8)

But in the greater scheme of things, the brothers were

blameless. They had no control over their rage, no way to question the hate-drenched thoughts that arose in them with the almost irresistibly seductive power that lust has. They were under the illusion that Joseph was the cause of their suffering; destroying the cause, they thought, would destroy the effect. Had they been better listeners, they would have understood why it turned out so badly for Cain: how his brother's blood continued to cry out from the ground and how his punishment, inflicted from the inside, felt greater than he could bear.

One last detail: Cain's famous question "Am I my brother's keeper?" has two equally valid answers. It requires a good deal of practice to discover where the yes fits and where the no.

The Errand

ONE DAY JACOB TOLD JOSEPH to see how the brothers were doing and bring him a report. Joseph blithely went off on his errand. His willful ignorance is easy to understand, but what about Jacob's? *He* certainly knew about brotherly rage; he had fled from the rage of his own brother, Esau, who had vowed to kill him after he found out that Jacob had cheated him out of the Blessing. Shouldn't Jacob have been more prudent now?

Well, in hindsight, yes, of course. But the fact is that he never thought Joseph was in danger. For one thing, the brothers had known better than to show their true feelings to him, so he hadn't been exposed to their fuming and gnashing of teeth. For another thing, in spite of his worries, he felt that Joseph was somehow protected. After all, not only was he one of Abraham's great-grandsons, he was the chosen among the chosen, a being of such beauty and brightness that he seemed invulnerable to earthly sorrows. Even the death of his mother, when he was six, hadn't affected him for more than a few weeks. He had cried himself empty every day, and then the grief was over, and he returned to his usual cheerfulness, with the memory of his mother a gently fading beacon at the center of his heart.

"Here Comes the Dreamer"

IT WAS NOON WHEN JOSEPH arrived in Dothan, where his brothers were tending their flocks. In the meadows there were a number of stone cisterns, which were used for gathering and storing water during the rainy season.

Simeon was the first to see him. "Look, here comes the dreamer," he said. "Now is our chance: let's kill him and throw him into one of these pits and say that a wild beast ate him. Then we'll see what good his dreams have done him."

The brothers all nodded in approval. Some of them laughed bitterly. (Judah, the only one whose hatred hadn't reached the boiling point, was in a different meadow, tending to a newborn lamb.)

As Joseph caught sight of them in the distance, he smiled. He was happy to arrive, and he thought they would be happy too. He couldn't parse the angry faces as he drew near. Simeon and Levi ran up and pinned his arms behind him. Someone was shouting, and before he knew it, his coat was torn off, then his tunic, and someone was hitting him in the face, and his mouth was bleeding. They were dragging him by the feet now. His head bumped along the ground. There were shouts and hoots all around him. Then he was falling. His right shoulder slammed against a wall, he lay stretched out on a rock, his head ached, there was a burning in his shoulder, suddenly the light dimmed, and he was alone in the shadows.

In the Pit

AT FIRST, HE WAS TOO SORE and frightened to move. He kept drifting in and out of consciousness, and he lost track of time. Was it only for hours that he had been lying here on the cold stone slab, or had it been for days? He heard some animal groaning, and he was frightened again. Then he realized that the animal was him.

As the pain subsided a bit, he was able to think. Why had his brothers done this to him? How could they be so cruel? How could they not see who he was?—the chosen one, the salvation of them all. He felt sad, angry, and bewildered. Nothing made sense.

Then, in the midst of his confusion, a glimmer of insight. Something he had done had so deeply offended his brothers that they wanted to kill him. Was it something, or was it everything—his whole way of being? Across the endless shivering hours, he could see himself from the outside, as the pampered favorite who sits at the right hand of the father, expecting the whole world to come worship at his feet. He was appalled. His heart ached at the arrogance of it and at his foolish sense of entitlement. He realized that he was entitled to nothing, not even his own life.

Naked, chilled, bruised, bloodcaked, terrified, stinking of urine and feces, he prayed not for forgiveness but for a little understanding of how he had gotten himself into such an unholy mess. He prayed for a little humility, which, if he ever emerged alive, he could follow through the night, as a caravan follows the North Star.

Learning Humility

"THE WAY UP AND THE WAY DOWN are one and the same," wrote an ancient philosopher. The stone cistern where Joseph lay was the womb of his transformation. He had to descend to the depths of himself and stay there, in that inner darkness, without refuge, without hope. This was the only path that could lead him upward. Then he had to find his way through a world of paradox, where exile is homecoming, slavery is freedom, and not knowing is the ultimate wisdom.

No one, of course, wants to suffer. And yet the fortunate among us manage to learn from our suffering what can be learned nowhere else. We become—clearly, joyously—aware of the cause of all suffering. Instead of sleep, the remembered pain drips into the heart, and an understanding dawns on us, even against our will, that there is a violent grace that shapes our ends. Humility follows as a natural result. We learn how to lose control. We discover that we never had it in the first place.

Humility looks very ordinary. It's hello and goodbye. At

first, it may seem like dying. What you were so proud of when you were flying high, you now recognize as selfish; it falls apart under scrutiny, and there is a profound change that takes place within you. There is no humiliation or shame in any of this. It's total surrender to what is. You discover that you have let go into an intelligence that is incomparably vaster than yours, and it's the gentlest, most comfortable feeling. You stand in what's left of you, and you die to self, and you keep on dying. It's like a tree that lets go of its leaves. That beautiful clothing has fallen away, and the tree just stands there in the cold of winter, totally exposed, totally surrendered.

Celebration

THE BROTHERS SAT DOWN TO EAT, on blankets they had spread on the grass. The flocks and herds were nearby. It was a cool day, but not cold enough for a fire.

They passed around the bread and cheese and goatskins of wine. Laughter; joking. Simeon said that the pit was an excellent place to dream in. Levi said that if Joseph was such a great dreamer, he could dream himself a staircase to heaven, or at least a staircase to the top of the pit. Everyone laughed.

In the silence between the jokes, they could hear Joseph's voice. "Save me," it whimpered.

"Let's see if God comes to save him," Zebulun said.

When Judah returned, his brothers told him what they had done. Judah was appalled. He realized what a devastating blow to Jacob the boy's death would be. He hated Joseph almost as much as the others did, but this was not the way. They couldn't do this to their father. He wanted to object, but he realized that nothing he might say would help. Their rage was out of control, and if he made himself their enemy now, they wouldn't listen to him later. Now was not the time to intervene.

Levi passed him the wineskin and told him not to be so stuffy. Relax, drink some wine, celebrate with them. What they had done was only right. The arrogant little prick deserved it.

A Gradual Letting Go

FOR A DAY AND A NIGHT—for days and nights, it seemed, as he drifted in and out of consciousness—Joseph lay in the pit, struggling with the realization that had dawned on him. The cold, filth, and physical pain were negligible in comparison with the moral pain he was feeling. Memories of his arrogance and unkindness toward his brothers flickered through his mind and made him heartsick. He was deeply ashamed of himself. It felt as if he had become Adam, in the story his father had told him so many times, and had eaten the fruit of the Tree of the Knowledge of Good and Evil, and it was a good thing, because suddenly his eyes were opened, and he knew that he was naked before God, before himself, stripped of all defense and justification. How could he have been so self-absorbed, such a sleepwalker? And where had his sense of chosenness led him but to this great sadness, which sat on his heart now like the weight of the sorry world?

He needed to make amends to his brothers—that was clear. But how? An apology seemed like a poor kind of restitution.

Besides, they would be too enraged to listen. They would see it as an attempt to talk his way out of danger. Anyway, the point was moot. He might be left to die here. He might be dragged out and beaten to death.

The shame burned inside him. *Forgive me*, he prayed, not to God but to his brothers, though he knew this was absurd. There was no way out. There were no solutions. There was nothing to do, nothing to pray but *May Your will be done*. He found himself sitting up now, with his back against one of the pit's stone walls. Overhead, the stars looked on in their frigid brilliance.

May Your will be done. But there was something very odd about the prayer. Wasn't it too an act of arrogance? Who was he to be telling God what should or shouldn't happen? Of *course* God's will would be done. How could it not? Everything that happened *was* God's will, or else it wouldn't have happened. You would have to be dull indeed if you didn't realize this. Had his brothers acted against God's will? It was insane even to think it. So, strange as it sounded, it was God who had thrown him into this pit. It was God who would let him live now or die. His brothers ultimately had nothing to do with it; they were just God's instruments. And he himself—think what he might, do what he might—could do nothing but God's will. *Not I, but You*, he thought. *Not what I want, but what You want. I am not doing any of this, nor are my brothers. Whatever we think we are doing, we are all doing what is best in Your sight. We are all doing Your will, dear Lord, because we are all the work of Your hands.*

This conclusion was not reasoned out. It came to him in a flash. It was not an idea; it was a certainty.

All the shame and sorrow he had been feeling began to dissipate, as if the sun were beginning to shine out from behind a layer of impenetrable fog. Even more: he began to be aware of—could it be?—a sense of elation rising in his chest. Was life really this simple? Could what had happened actually be something good?

What he had been struggling against was now letting go of him, or he of it. He had been trying to fight against the current of reality, and now he was riding it, his mind a sleek skiff in the onrushing river, letting it take him wherever it wished. The direction didn't matter. His life didn't matter. All that mattered was the letting go.

Caravan

THE NEXT MORNING, AS THE brothers were finishing their breakfast, they saw a caravan of Ishmaelites growing larger in the distance.

"What would we gain by killing Joseph?" Judah said to his brothers as the caravan approached. "Why not sell him to these merchants? There's no need to harm him. After all, he is our own flesh and blood."

So they pulled Joseph out of the pit, and they washed him and gave him a clean robe and some bread and wine. By the time the merchants arrived, he looked (barely) presentable.

The Ishmaelites

THE ISHMAELITES WERE ON THEIR way from Gilead to Egypt. They were descendants of Ishmael, the son of Abraham and his slave Hagar—a boy who, as prophesied, grew up to be as free as a wild donkey, his hand against everyone and everyone's hand against him. (This was no surprise, since he had grown up seeing his mother constantly abused by his stepmother.)

Ishmael's descendants were still somewhat wild, but in the course of the generations they had evolved from bandits and raiders to canny businessmen. They were dressed in kaffiyehs and white robes, with swords and daggers hanging from their leather belts. On their camels' backs they had placed manageable loads of spices, balm, and resin, which were highly valued in Egypt as medicine, cosmetics, and embalming aids. They also earned some profit on the side by buying children at very low prices from impoverished Canaanite farmers, who were only too glad to earn a few shekels by getting rid of the extra mouths.

The caravan halted. Its leader got down from his camel and wished the brothers peace, then asked them if they had any merchandise to sell. (There was no need for an interpreter, since the Ishmaelite language was a close cousin of Hebrew.) Thrilled that the merchants had arrived at such an opportune moment, the brothers said that in fact they had a very attractive slave for sale. The Ishmaelites inspected Joseph, huddled together, and offered twenty shekels for him. Twenty shekels was, the brothers knew, a ridiculously low price for such a handsome and intelligent young man, but haggling would have been entirely beside the point. So they accepted.

The Ishmaelites were disappointed. They had fastened feed bags onto their camels' snouts and tied up the animals' callused knees for a morning-long session of negotiations. The subtle back-and-forth movement of the price was one of the joys of the merchant's profession, and it seemed like an insult to have their first price accepted, as if the Hebrews didn't think them worthy opponents. But they quickly realized that something fishy was going on, something that probably had to do with the young man's bruises, which were, the brothers explained, the result of a bad fall. And the price was remarkable enough to make up for the loss of their sport. So they rode off chuckling to themselves. The new slave would be worth at least two hundred silver coins when they arrived in Egypt.

Did you notice that Joseph was silent during this transaction? He could have cried out against his brothers and, with his considerable eloquence, tried to move the Ishmaelites' hearts to take him home, where his wealthy father would pay them a large ransom. But he didn't utter a word. He realized again, with an awe that made protest seem foolish, that it was not his brothers but some vast intelligence that had cast him into the pit and brought him up out of it, and was about to send him, bound hand and foot, on the winding path down into the black land of Egypt.*

---

* Rabbi Yehoshua bar Dosa of Shunem said, "Joseph knew that it was God who had cast him down and brought him up. As it is said, 'The Lord brought me up out of the horrible pit.'" (Ps. 40:2)

Beyond Comfort

AFTER THE CARAVAN LEFT, the brothers slaughtered a kid and soaked Joseph's coat in its blood. As you may remember, Jacob had slaughtered a kid to carry out his deception when he stole the Blessing from his brother, Esau, and here is another kid and another deception, and in the Judah and Tamar story there will be a third. Is this divine irony? Poetic justice? Or simple coincidence, in an age when slaughtering a kid was like our going to the refrigerator? The brothers took a visceral pleasure in soaking Joseph's coat in the blood. Its whole surface turned dull. The vibrant colors disappeared. The two angels stiffened.

They drove the flocks and herds home. When they arrived, they brought the coat to their father and said, with hypocritically troubled faces, "Father, we found this. It looks like your son's."

"Oh dear God," Jacob cried out, "my son's coat! A wild beast ate him! Joseph is torn to pieces!" and he sank to the ground, sobbing. When he was able to stand up, he tore his clothes and dressed in sackcloth.

Leah, the concubines, the daughters-in-law, and Benjamin all tried to comfort him. The other sons added some double-edged words. Appalled at the intensity of their father's grief, they now had pity added to their witches' brew of rage, resentment, and guilt.

But Jacob refused to be comforted. He had no way of reaching a comfort that could encompass this devastation. None of his close encounters with the divine had the slightest effect on his despair—not even the night at Bethel, when in a dream trance he had seen a staircase rising from the ground all the way to heaven, with angels moving up and down it, as if to a solemn music that he could not hear; not even the wrestling match at the ford of the Jabbok, when he had struggled with and prevailed over God, if God was that burly stranger with wide-set ox eyes that never blinked. "I will never stop mourning," he wailed. "I will mourn for my son every hour of every day, until I myself go down to the grave."

He had lost his beloved for the second time, and neither memory nor prayer could lift him out of the mental pit he had fallen into.

Leah

IT BROKE LEAH'S HEART to see him like this.

She had grown into a woman of deep feelings, from the rather shallow, unpleasant girl of long ago. When she was young, she had felt constantly outshone by Rachel, the Lamb, especially after Rachel and Jacob had fallen in love, and during the seven years he had served for his beloved she had retreated into the haughty-young-lady-of-good-family role. In comparison with her vivacious younger sister, she was dull—a dullness of spirit that you could see in her eyes; some kind of mental fog seemed to have rolled in behind them. She had also manifested at least one of her father's more unpleasant traits, which she was embarrassed to recall: a moral insensitivity beneath the social veneer, a merchant's way of sizing people up and figuring out how he could get the most out of them for the least expenditure.

Since she had been a dutiful daughter, she had gone along with Laban's duplicity in substituting her for the rightful bride. But she had been shaken by Jacob's anguish and rage in the morning; she'd had no idea that he would be so wounded by her very presence. And in the following years, though he managed to satisfy her sexually, she craved affection from him, and she felt demoralized at its absence from her life. She saw how he and her sister doted on each other, and it hurt her, since she loved Jacob too. Even though she was as fertile as a woman can be—and in those days fertility was a woman's glory—nothing she did could win the love of her husband. If it hadn't been for her children and the love she felt for them, she would have been crushed by the weight of her loneliness. After Joseph was born, she was also saddened by Jacob's blatant preference for him over her own children, though she understood it. Joseph was a remarkable child.

Then Rachel died at the age of forty-two. Leah thought that this would be some kind of release for her, but it wasn't. In spite of her jealousy, she loved her sister. She loved Jacob too, and it was impossible to see him suffer so greatly and not want to take him into her arms. But he refused all comforting—brushed her away, said that he couldn't bear it—and in the end she could come up with nothing to help him but her tenderness, unproffered but always there. She understood how important Joseph was to Jacob, how he was the only thing standing between that good man and utter despair. She tried to explain this to her sons, but whenever she began, they would interrupt her with their fiery grievances.

When Joseph disappeared, Jacob fell apart. It truly broke Leah's heart to see him cowering before reality like a beaten child, unable to get out of bed in the morning, unable to talk, unable to eat, sobbing in his tent for hours at a time. This went on for months, and she thought he might never be able to crawl back up to the world of daylight from whatever pit of Sheol he had fallen into, wailing in the darkness with the rest of the disconsolate dead. Over the months and years, though, Jacob came back to life, if "life" means a joyless effort to endure each day.

There wasn't much that Leah could do for him. Sometimes he would let her hold his hand. She knew better than to say anything unless he spoke to her first.

She also sensed that her sons must have had some connection with Joseph's death. She had been there when they brought the blood-soaked coat to Jacob, and she could tell that they were hiding something. But she was afraid to ask them about it. She didn't want to know if—how—they were involved. Her task was difficult enough now: waiting always on the edge of alertness to provide Jacob with her meager comfort. She didn't have the heart to deal with her sons as well.

II.
Judah and Tamar

In Lieu of a Digression on Digressions

OUR STORY IS GETTING RICHER all the time, but I need to break off from the main plot now, gentle reader, and move on to the tale-within-a-tale of Judah and Tamar, because that is how our storyteller, who had a keen instinct for suspense, structured his narrative. If I knew you were interested, I might have inserted a digression on digressions here, tracing the history of literary detours, from the Ishtar story in *Gilgamesh* through *The Iliad* and *The Odyssey* to *The Thousand and One Nights* to *Don Quixote* and *Tristram Shandy* and *Jacques le fataliste* to Tolstoy and Proust and beyond: a glorious history, which, however, needn't detain us. Those of you who can't wait for the next installment of the Joseph story are welcome to skip to page 93. (I have to warn you, though, that you'll miss an essential element in the formation of Judah's character.) The rest of you should keep reading, as long as you realize that Judah is about to step into a metaphysical time warp. Time—that very elastic quality of our perceptual apparatus, in the illusion of which we live our lives—slows to a snail crawl now in the world of

Joseph, and during the two weeks when he is being transported to Egypt, twenty-two years pass in Judah's world: he marries, fathers three sons, and all three reach marriageable age. Then, just as suddenly as he had left home, there he is again in Hebron with his father, mother, and ten remaining brothers, an older and wiser man, bringing with him one son and a splendid, very pregnant daughter-in-law, whom we never hear of again.

Judah Departs

SO JUDAH LEFT HEBRON AND HEADED north, with his flocks and herds, into the time warp. He wanted to establish a new life for himself. His brothers' company was painful. It constantly reminded him of the crime he had committed, though he didn't need their presence as a reminder; often, as he lay in bed at night trying to seek refuge in sleep, he would see images of Joseph after he had been dragged out of the pit, with his wounds still raw and ugly. And the silence to which Judah felt bound, the complicity for which he thought he would never be able to forgive himself, stuck in his throat like a chunk of meat that he could neither swallow nor cough out.

It was all difficult for him, but the worst of it was having to live so close to his father's grief. The old man was a fragment of his former self. Misery had hollowed out his eyes and made the flesh wither on his bones. On seeing him, Judah would be overwhelmed with guilt and pity. He wanted to say, "Don't grieve, Father. It will all come right in the end," but the words would have been a self-indulgence, with no reality to back them up. The only honest thing he could have said was, "We lied to you, Father. We sold Joseph into slavery. He may still be alive." But would saying this be a kindness? Or would it break his father's heart and push him right into the abyss?

Telling the truth wasn't a choice, though; it wasn't his decision to make. Or was this thought too a mere excuse for cowardice? Was loyalty to his brothers a virtue? Was it a betrayal of his father, or a way to keep his father alive, or both?

The whole matter was too complex and humiliating to contemplate. Better to pull up stakes, move to a place where no one had ever heard of his family, and begin again.

Tamar

HE SETTLED TO THE NORTHWEST, near Adullam, one of the royal cities. There he married the daughter of a Jebusite named Shua. The marriage was a good one; in fact, the two of them were so compatible that Judah felt no need for an additional wife or even for a concubine.

His wife gave birth to three sons: Er, Onan, and Shelah. But her health was fragile, and after Shelah was born they decided to avoid a fourth pregnancy. So they made love only when Judah's desire overran its banks, and they were extremely careful when they did.

After Er grew up, Judah chose a wife for him, a Hivite woman named Tamar. At the time he couldn't have guessed what a remarkable woman he had chosen. But he had seen enough of Tamar to have a sense of her character: honest, firm, respectful, affectionate, kind to animals, an excellent daughter and sister to her large family. She was like her name: תָּמָר (tamár), a date palm, tall, strong, and in all probability, with her womanly figure, fruitful; chances were that she would bear many children. He had spoken with her about her life, a simple one of devotion to her family, and about her sense of the divine. She was an idolater, of course, like all her people. But she wasn't one of those girls who were enthralled with the worship of Ishtar, which to his mind was a mere excuse for licentiousness. She knew what was proper and what wasn't. When she spoke of Baal's creative power and of how he wishes humans to treat one another with decency and respect, Judah felt that she was not irredeemably lost in her pagan delusions. She listened to him with fascination when he told her that there is only one God, but her loyalty to her parents made it unthinkable for her to abandon her beliefs. Still, she was teachable, and at worst, he thought, she would turn out to be a loving wife and mother.

But Er died suddenly. Shortly afterward, Judah said to Onan, "Go and fulfill your obligation as a brother-in-law, as the law requires: lie with your brother's widow and produce a child for him."

Onan had sex with Tamar three times, but he couldn't force himself to produce a child for his brother. Clearly, there had been some serious unresolved issues between them. Every time he entered Tamar and began thrusting, he thought of Er, and so much resentment boiled up inside him that he felt compelled to withdraw and ejaculate onto the ground. It had nothing to do with Tamar, whom he liked well enough. But he was damned if he was going to give that dead son of a bitch the satisfaction.

Then Onan too died suddenly. The youngest son, Shelah, was only twelve. Judah said to Tamar, "Go back to your father's house until my third son grows up." He assumed that Tamar was cursed and that if he did the right thing—instructed his son to impregnate her as soon as he was old enough, as the law required—Shelah too would die. He was choosing the lesser of the two evils: the sin of not fulfilling his obligation to Tamar, rather than the sin of costing the boy his life.

The proper thing to do, of course, would have been to tell her about his fear. But he felt too guilty for that.

Sheepshearing

THEN JUDAH'S WIFE DIED. She had been ill for some time, too ill to make love with him, so in addition to his grief, he was feeling sexually deprived. After the period of mourning was over, he decided to go to Timnah for the sheepshearing, together with his friend Hirah.

Sheepshearing was a time of celebration, thanksgiving, and revelry. People ate a lot and drank a lot of wine, and there were parties in the tents of the richest magnates, who would order priestesses of Ishtar to be brought in from Ekron or Beth-Shemesh, women whose lives were dedicated to the sacred mystery of sexual union and who, in opening themselves to the anonymous men who patronized them, became incarnations of the goddess and with their own bodies reenacted the cosmic marriage. The poet of *Gilgamesh*, Sîn-lēqi-unninni, considered these sacred prostitutes to be one of the principal glories of civilization, and he wrote of them with glowing civic pride:

the lovely priestesses standing before
the temple of Ishtar, chatting and laughing,
flushed with sexual joy, and ready
to serve men's pleasure, in honor of the goddess.

On the roads there were also freelance harlots who did business at the festival. Most of the shepherds weren't picky about the distinction between sacred and profane.

A Desperate Plan

JUDAH'S IMPENDING TRIP made the rounds of local gossip. Eventually, a neighbor mentioned it to Tamar.

She was twenty and Shelah fourteen, certainly old enough to perform his fraternal duty, and still there was no word from her father-in-law. It had been a long time since she last heard from him. She knew what was in his mind: that she was to blame for the sudden deaths of his two older sons. She had no way to prove that she wasn't. All she could do, if he should ever blame her, was fall at his feet and beg him to fulfill his obligation, and even that seemed less and less of a possibility. She knew not only that she had an imperious need for children but that it was her legal right. Since Judah refused to cooperate, she would have to take the matter into her own hands.

As she was doing the laundry one day, a plan sprang into her mind. It was dangerous; it made her shiver with dread. It could also be seen as a revolt against her father-in-law's authority, and because of the offense it might give him and the whole community, she was extremely reluctant to proceed.

But what else could she do? However frightened she was, she felt that she would rather die than remain mute and childless.

So she took off her widow's clothes, put on her best robe, walked to Enayim, covered her face with a veil, and sat down at the entrance gate, on the road to Timnah.

The Pledge

WHEN JUDAH SAW HER, he thought that she was a harlot, since her face was veiled and she was sitting alone at the entrance gate. Providentially, it was the custom of Canaanite harlots to cover their faces. This gave them a certain mysterious je ne sais quoi and allowed even beauty-challenged girls to ply a brisk trade. The men were willing to forgo the delights of kissing; they were primarily interested in breasts and genitals anyway, and in the kinky pleasures they didn't dare ask of their virtuous, Baal-fearing wives.

To understand the situation better, you should know that during the patriarchal era, sacred prostitution was accepted by all cultures in the Near East. (This status quo lasted for another thousand years, until it was attacked by uncomprehending prophets such as Hosea and Ezekiel.) So according to the ethics of his time, Judah was doing nothing wrong here. It was perfectly kosher for a Jewish man to visit a prostitute, though it was forbidden for a Jewish woman to *be* a prostitute.

Judah walked up to Tamar and said, "Let me come into you."

Tamar said, "What will you pay me?"

"I will send you a kid from my flock," he said. This was the going rate. Being a fair man, Judah didn't want to offend her by haggling over the price.

Tamar breathed a sigh of relief. Her whole plan hinged on Judah's promising a payment. If he had insisted on paying her immediately (in silver, for example), the business would have been complete, and she would have had no proof that he was her child's father.

"All right," she said, "but leave me a pledge until you send it."

Judah said, "What pledge?"

"Your seal and the staff you are holding." The staff had carvings on it that identified its owner, and the cylinder seal, perforated and worn on a cord around the neck, was used to sign contracts. In those days no respectable man would be seen in public without one.

So he gave them to her, and they had sex behind the bushes.

Behind the Bushes

JUDAH WAS A GENEROUS LOVER. He took his time. He enjoyed giving pleasure as much as he enjoyed receiving it, and he made sure that Tamar was satisfied. In this she counted herself fortunate, especially since it was in all probability the last time there would be any sex in her life.

But pleasure wasn't the point. She loved her father-in-law, and the tenderness with which he touched her was a revelation, given Er's clumsiness and the bitter onslaughts of Onan. It wouldn't have mattered greatly, though, if Judah had been a selfish lover. She was there for one purpose only: to collect his seed.

The veil was dense enough to hide her features, but not so dense that she couldn't see through it. As she lay back, knees raised, robe hiked up onto her belly, his penis thrusting slowly inside her, she examined his face. He was looking down at her with a smile. She couldn't know what he was feeling, but from the look in his eyes it seemed like gratitude—almost, to her amazement, like love. After their climaxes, she noticed tears at the corners of his eyes as he held her in his arms and stroked her hair. Then he stood up, extended his right hand to help her off the ground, nodded in acknowledgment, and thanked her, his voice filled with emotion.

When she went home, she took off the veil and robe and put on her widow's clothes again. She had gotten through the difficult part. The rest was in the hands of Baal. All she had to do was wait.

Where Is the Harlot?

JUDAH SENT HIS FRIEND HIRAH, with a kid on a leash, to redeem the pledge from the woman. Hirah went all over the neighborhood asking, "Where is the harlot who was sitting by the roadside at Enayim?"

"What harlot?" everyone said. "There was no harlot here."

Finally he gave up and went back to Judah.

"I looked all over," he said. "I asked everyone. But I couldn't find her."

Judah said, "Well, she can keep the pledge. If I go on looking for her, I'll make myself a laughingstock. My conscience is clear. I kept my promise. I can't help it if you weren't able to find her."

The First Trimester

ALREADY, BEHIND THE BUSHES at the entrance gate to Enayim, Tamar knew she was pregnant. This was not wishful thinking. She felt it in her body. She was certain.

So during the following weeks and months, she wasn't surprised at her breasts' sensitivity, the crankiness that could bring her to tears at the slightest upset, the sometimes baffling, sometimes delicious, fatigue, the craving for odd combinations of food, and the sense of smell heightened, it seemed, beyond the realm of the human. *Yes*, she would tell herself, *it is happening, just as I knew it would. My body is changing around the child. It is changing* for *the child.*

These were the quiet days, the days of calm, when she could go about her daily chores with the awareness that no one knew what had happened. People would know soon enough.

The Hivites, like all Canaanites, honored sex for its own sake and condoned sacred prostitution, and secular prostitution too, for that matter, as long as it was practiced by unmarried women. But they were severe in punishing unfaithful wives and widows; the penalty was death by fire. Tamar didn't think that her family would betray her, even though their sense of piety would urge them to. But eventually someone would notice. She couldn't stay in the house all the time, and sooner or later someone would see her at the market or at the well and would denounce her to Judah, the head of her husband's family. She could be as certain of this as of the sun's rising in the east.

So she would be brought before Judah, and he would be forced to condemn her to death. It couldn't happen in any other way. But she felt no fear. She had staked her life on Judah's probity, and she knew how he would react when she showed him the seal and staff. There was no chance in the world that he would disown them. For him to deny responsibility would be as if one fine morning the sun decided to rise in the west.

She didn't consider herself particularly brave. In devising her act of trickery, she had simply been claiming what was rightfully hers, according to the laws of man and of Baal. And there was no risk. She knew Judah. They had talked many times about right and wrong—or rather, he had talked and she had listened respectfully, admiringly. He had a lofty mind, she thought, and though she would never dream of renouncing her family's faith, she thrilled when he spoke of his single God, blissful and alone behind the curtain of appearances, who had created heaven and earth and the moral law in the human heart. The possibility that her father-in-law would be capable of doing anything unworthy brought a smile to her lips.

Denouement

ABOUT THREE MONTHS LATER, one of Tamar's neighbors said to Judah, "Your daughter-in-law is a whore, and she has gotten herself pregnant from her whoring." This neighbor was a notorious busybody, and Judah at first refused to believe her. But soon there was another report, then another.

So he had Tamar brought before the town elders, and it was clear that the reports were true. "It saddens me to say it," he told the elders, "but according to the law she must be burned." This conclusion may seem very harsh, but if Tamar was pregnant, she had to be guilty, and it was not only Judah's right but his duty to condemn her to death. It never occurred to him to look beyond the evidence, which seemed indisputable. He had expected much more from her, and he was ashamed that he had been so wrong about her character.

They stood in the market square, with her family and a crowd of townspeople in attendance. Some of them were shocked into silence, but many, especially the women, were vocal. "Slut!" they shouted. "Whore!" And to Judah: "Burn her!"

Tamar stood calmly, as if the death sentence had nothing to do with her. After Judah read it out, he asked if she had anything to say.

"Sir," she answered, "the man who got me pregnant is the owner of this seal and this staff. See if you recognize whose they are."

The courage and delicacy of her response have echoed through Jewish history. The medieval commentator Rashi wrote, "She did not want to embarrass him by saying, 'You are the man who got me pregnant.' She thought, *If he confesses, good. If he doesn't confess, let them burn me alive, but I will not embarrass him.* From this example our sages concluded, 'It is better to be cast into a fiery furnace than to shame your neighbor in public.'"

As for Judah, the situation would have been shameful only if there had been something to hide. But in patronizing a harlot, he had done nothing immoral.

He recognized the seal and staff as his own. Then he remembered the encounter at Enayim. Ah. So it had been Tamar. He blushed at his delinquency. Being a righteous man, he bowed his head in acknowledgment and said, "This woman is in the right, and I am in the wrong, because I didn't give her to my youngest son."

It would have been easy for Judah to deny responsibility. He could have said, "Yes, I did have sex with you, one time. But how many other men have you slept with? How can I know that the child is mine?" But he didn't allow his mind to play such tricks on him. He immediately understood that

Tamar was a heroine, and with his acknowledgment he himself became a hero. In fact, he became, for the moment, a master of reality:

> When he makes a mistake, he realizes it.
> Having realized it, he admits it.
> Having admitted it, he corrects it.
> He considers those who point out his faults
> as his most benevolent teachers.
> He thinks of his enemy
> as the shadow that he himself casts.

He was filled with admiration for his daughter-in-law's resoluteness in the face of the obstacle he had created. It was clear that he needed to make amends to her in every way possible, to take her in and treat her as a beloved daughter, and to honor her for a courage and strength of character that far exceeded his own.* Needless to say, he never had sex with her again.

It was while she was pregnant that he moved back to Hebron. Neither Jacob nor anyone else in the family realized that he had been gone for twenty-two years, since in their world just six days had passed; every day of theirs was three and two-thirds years of Judah's. They were too polite to ask for explanations about how he had aged so radically or about Shelah and Tamar; and Judah, after his initial bewilderment at re-

---

* Rabbi Eleazar ben Yannai of Tiberias said, "Tamar is an example for the righteous of all nations. As it is said, 'The righteous shall flourish like Tamar.'" (Ps. 92:12)

turning home as a reverse Rip van Winkle, soon dismissed the subject from his mind.

When Tamar gave birth to twins, whom she named Perez and Zerah, Judah pronounced them to be the legitimate children of his eldest son, Er, her dead husband, fathered by himself. Nine generations later, in the line of Perez, Jesse begot David, who was to become king of Israel. After another twenty-seven generations (according to Matthew), or forty-two generations (according to Luke), Joseph of Nazareth begot Jesus.

The Jewish tradition shows a remarkable degree of tolerance for the apparent scandalousness of this line of descent. After all, not only was Tamar a Gentile, but both prostitution and incest (of a sort) were the necessary ingredients in her pregnancy. She is also honored in the Christian tradition, but in a fascinatingly oblique way. Here is how the Evangelist Matthew traces the lineage of Jesus: "Abraham begot Isaac, Isaac begot Jacob, Jacob begot Judah and his brothers, Judah begot Perez and Zerah out of Tamar, . . . Salmon begot Boaz out of Rahab, Boaz begot Obed out of Ruth, . . . David begot Solomon out of Uriah's wife . . ." The peculiar feature in his list is the mention of the four women, each of whom had something sexually irregular about her: Rahab was a prostitute and the madam of a brothel; Ruth got her second husband by an act of immodesty, if not solicitation; and Bathsheba began her relationship with David in adultery. Why did Matthew insert them into his genealogy? (In Luke's divergent genealogy, no women are mentioned.) The likeliest explanation is that he wanted to excuse the pregnant and unwed Mary by these implied analogies.

Now we can return to *our* Joseph, son of Jacob, great-grandson of Abraham. We rejoin him as he travels with the Ishmaelite caravan on its way down to the land of Egypt.

III.

In Potiphar's Palace

Sinai Journal

HOMER SAYS THAT A MAN LOSES half his soul on the day he becomes a slave. But Joseph's soul remained intact. What he had lost—his home and family, his dignity, his arrogance— was actually a gain. He had died to his old self and been reborn as someone more self-aware, more skeptical of his assumptions, a lover of the truth. He saw the world with curious eyes now. It wasn't necessarily a bad thing for him to be a slave, he realized. He had become the lowest of the low, an element, like water, content with the low places that people disdain. Life had accordingly become very simple. His job was to follow directions. Whatever someone in authority told him to do, he did. He was free of decisions, and he would soon be free of idleness as well. There was no feeling of humiliation in any of this. On the contrary, he was grateful to know exactly what his duty was at every moment.

The first day of the journey was uncomfortable, but once his bonds were untied, the Ishmaelites treated him decently. They fed him well; some of them even took a liking to him, particularly a young man named Tema. Tema talked to Kedar, the leader of the caravan, and Joseph was given a camel of his own to ride on.

✧

They entered the Sinai, the Land of Turquoise. Nothing on all sides but red granite and blue sky. On the first day, the flies sent their hospitality committee; they hovered around Joseph's legs, arms, and face and would not be shooed away. "This is the flavor of the desert," Tema said. "You get used to them."

✧

Falcons circled overhead. On both sides of the trail the caravan passed huge red granite boulders that looked like Henry Moore sculptures. Some of the boulders had names: "the Overturned Boat," "the House of the Lions," "the Two Rocks Talking." Tema, with a laugh: "They're talking because they like each other very much."

✧

Tema told him that in this heat it was important not to get dehydrated. So they stopped every few hours to drink water and rest in the shade.

✧

One day they found a boulder house beside a spring. Tema said that hunters would sit here and wait for ibexes, who have to drink at least once a day, unlike gazelles, who can go for days without water. The canyon was covered with wild mint, which had tiny purple flowers and was wonderfully fragrant. They gathered some for tea.

✧

Quails everywhere, whistling from wadi to wadi. Tema pointed out the occasional quail trap: three sticks propping up a rock.

✧

As the wadis became narrower, the landscape changed: willows, reeds. The caravan stopped for an hour, and Joseph, along with Tema and several other young men and boys, climbed down to twin pools, an upper and a lower one, next to a cliff shaded by willows. In this desert, water seemed like a miracle. It moved him beyond words. He dived into the upper pool. Freezing! When he climbed out and sat on the rocks to dry, he could see how deeply the dirt had caked into his skin.

✧

He thought of his father every day. He knew how devastated he must be. There was nothing Joseph could do about that.

Thinking of Jacob was a curious process. His image would appear in Joseph's mind arbitrarily, as he was on the camel or lying under his blanket at night. He saw the old man weeping or tearing his clothes in grief, and he would immediately react to that image with sorrow, pity, and a helpless sinking feeling in his stomach. But as soon as he became aware of this reaction—usually just a few moments had passed, though sometimes he got lost in his pity—he would remember that God's will was always done, that both he and his father were in the care of that vast intelligence. And then, for a while, the image of Jacob no longer made his heart ache.

❖

Sitting around the campfire one night, they talked about women. Tema to Joseph: "Everyone knows that women are smarter than men. The female ibex leads the herd and warns others of danger. If one of our young men is too wild, he usually settles down after he gets married. His wife says, 'You must provide for us.' She shows him the right way, and the young man stops his foolishness."

"On the other hand," Kedar said with a wry smile, "all trouble comes from women. Life is difficult with them and difficult without them. Look at the rocks: they're silent, unmoving. If there were no women, we'd be like these rocks. As it is, we go about from land to land so that we can provide for our wives."

Joseph looked at him with interest. Kedar was in his forties or fifties, his face baked by the sun, deep wrinkles in his forehead and around his eyes.

"With that attitude," Joseph asked, "how can you trust your wives?"

"Ah," Kedar said, "never trust a woman. Never even trust your own wives."

Joseph, puzzled: "Don't you love your wives?"

"Of course I do."

"But how can you love someone and not trust her?"

Kedar: "I love my three-year-old boy, but I wouldn't trust him with a camel."

The conversation moved to children. Kedar: "You must keep your children close to you. Children are your own flesh.

What happens to flesh, to meat, if you leave it somewhere and don't keep your eyes on it?"

Tema, like a good student: "It rots."

Kedar nodded. "So with children."

The young men and boys around the campfire listened attentively. This was how they learned the wisdom and the foolishness of their elders.

◇

After placing his blanket under a lone pomegranate tree, Joseph lay watching the shadow of the moon on the cliffs. A bat swooped down, feasting on insects attracted by the oil lamp. After an hour the moon rose. Then the first small trumpets of the mosquitoes.

He slapped at one on his right cheek. How annoying to have all this beauty interrupted! But then he considered his reaction. On the sixth day of the Creation, in the story that Jacob had delighted to tell him from as far back as he could remember, God had looked at the world and had said, "Behold, it is very good." Hadn't that sixth-day awareness continued until now, and wouldn't it continue until the end of time? Didn't God, even now, look at everything He had created and see that it was very good? What if even flies too, and ants and mosquitoes, had their purpose to fulfill and Joseph's annoyance was a missed opportunity to appreciate that? The mosquito, bless its little black heart—didn't it have its own peculiar beauty, when you stood apart from yourself as a human being? Wasn't its whine an essential note in the harmony of creation? Maybe there was nothing unnecessary or mistaken or evil in all the universe. Could that really be true?

✧

Another night. Wild donkeys—five, with two colts—were watching them from the hill above. Tema told Joseph that he had more than once lost food to wild donkeys. So he took the bread, dates, winter pears, dried meat, and other staples and placed them close to his blanket. "Their leader is planning to wait till we go to sleep," he said. "She thinks we'll leave the food unprotected. The gods tell us to be kind to animals, but enough is enough." Then he collected stones and arranged them in a pile beside him. Every now and then, when the donkeys got too close, he threw a stone at them.

All night, in and out of Joseph's dreams, the *clomp clomp* of donkey hooves.

Arrival in Egypt

RED BOATS ARE SAILING UNDER a turquoise sky. On shore, in the high-walled gardens, cats doze in the sun, skinny from eating lizards, and in rosemary and honeysuckle the bees labor like slaves.

This is the land of mud, where the dead are planted feet upward. How it will all turn out he cannot guess. He is free only to watch, to listen, to let his mind find its equilibrium in the pitch dark of itself.

Sold

EARLY AFTERNOON: A BREAK in the negotiations. One of Kedar's sons filled cups of burnished marl with honey-enhanced wine from Ashkelon and served them to the chief slave dealer and his assistants. As they drank, Kedar chatted with him in fluent but guttural Egyptian. The two men had been doing business for many years and respected each other. Each knew the other's best moves.

The price for Joseph had been more or less determined during the first minute of the examination. The slave dealer had uttered some perfunctory grumbles about Joseph's height, but the rare beauty of his face and body was undeniable, and Joseph's intelligence and wit shone through their brief conversation. (Tema served as interpreter.) Kedar had begun at three hundred silver coins and had slowly, deliciously, and with many apparent scruples, much moral dignity, let the price, little by little, drop. It was at two hundred seventy now, after four hours of passionate dealing. It wouldn't be allowed to fall below two hundred fifty. Both men knew that.

Four other slaves had already been sold—three scrawny Amorite peasant boys and a girl—at eleven silver coins for the lot. The process had taken less than half an hour.

Joseph looked on and listened. He loved the sound of the Egyptian language, the subtly nuanced consonants, the uvular trill of the *r*, which sounded like birdsong, the flowing movement of the long, leisurely sentences, so different from the blunt forthrightness of his native Hebrew. He couldn't tell what was going on, except that Kedar and his adversary were enjoying themselves immensely. From time to time they turned to him and pointed, as if they were arguing over the precise monetary value of a shapely leg or an elegant eyebrow.

He felt no apprehension about his future status, whatever that might be, because by now he had learned not to think himself into a future. He was well aware that he might be sold to a callous or even a cruel owner, who might beat him or work him to death. But he didn't let the images connect, to frighten himself with possibilities. For all he knew, the worst of this experience was already over. He was excited to see what would come next.

After three more hours, they struck a deal. Both sides were pleased. Kedar, having made sure that the coins added up to two hundred sixty, eased them into a large leather purse. Then he rode off with his caravan to sell the rest of the merchandise.

The slave dealer brought his purchases to his master, a eunuch named Potiphar, who was the chief officer of Pharaoh's bodyguard.

Potiphar

POTIPHAR WAS A TALL MAN with a placid temperament, having been gelded at the age of ten. He had been bred as a courtier, and he was everything a courtier should be: a witty conversationalist, an elegant dancer, an adept at card games, a hunter, a drinker, a bureaucrat, and a shrewd politician, who knew just when a compliment would delight or a snub sting. Because he was immune to sexual indiscretions, and therefore less vulnerable to palace intrigues, he was considered to be particularly trustworthy. He had known Pharaoh since childhood (they were second cousins) and had been rewarded for his faithful service with a palace in the city, a country estate, and a wife from an old noble family, a woman of superior education, whose ambition was gratified by her husband's steady rise in court circles. She was comfortable with her enforced chastity, not missing what she had never had. Looking beautiful, basking in the favors of Pharaoh, and being talked about with admiration and envy by everyone who mattered—that was enough, she thought.

Joseph's Ascent

POTIPHAR SOON BECAME AWARE of Joseph's extraordinary talents. The young man, assigned to table duty, was so handsome and graceful that one couldn't help noticing him. The formal dinners afforded no opportunity for closer observation, so Potiphar summoned the slave to his office, a spacious, high-ceilinged room lined with gods made of alabaster, porphyry, and marble. As he interviewed Joseph, he was dazzled by his eloquence and the breadth of his understanding. He spent more than an hour with him, and he was sorry to see him leave. (By this time Joseph's Egyptian was more than adequate for a conversation, though he would sometimes stumble over the conventional pieties that ornamented the language like the trills of a Baroque melody.)

To say that Potiphar took a liking to him would be an understatement. Potiphar's heart was touched. He felt rejuvenated in the young man's presence. He wanted, then longed, to see more of him. Soon he made him his personal attendant and gave him an Egyptian name: Meri-Amun, Beloved of Amun, the Hidden One, who by this time was identified with the sun god Ra.

The promotions to chief secretary and majordomo happened quickly and naturally; there was no grumbling among the other slaves at the barbarian's heady rise, since he was universally esteemed; the master's affection didn't seem excessive nor his confidence misplaced. Under Joseph's direction, daily business began to take care of itself with minimal stress on the whole staff. Everyday chores became a pleasure for them, and throughout the palace there was a perpetual hum of contentment in the air, as if the great goddess Bast were curled up on the rooftop, purring.

The Golden Touch

JOSEPH OBVIOUSLY HAD THE GOLDEN TOUCH. Everyone could see it, from the chief steward to the lowest-ranking scullery maid. It was not only his extraordinary intelligence that made his work prosper, or his mastery of detail, or his affability, which gave pleasure to all the slaves who worked with, and later for, him. There was something else. People called it prescience. They thought that some god must be whispering into his ear during the wee hours of the night.

It was, of course, nothing of the sort. Joseph couldn't see into the future, but he could, with his meticulous focus, see into the interstices of the present, out of which success and failure are born. It was like moving through a dense crowd, not thinking about where to go or how to get there, but letting his own movement find the gaps between bodies, letting it effortlessly flow through them until, as if his path were one long exhalation, he found himself on the other side of the room. He trusted this unthinking movement. It was the opposite of the arrogance that had been his default mode in his former life. The great things he was destined for were none of his business. His business was to see where the openings were and to glide through them.

The Great Commandment

WHAT PEOPLE SENSED IN JOSEPH was a wisdom that was actually a mode of love. Through his death and rebirth, he had found a way to live the still-unhanded-down Great Commandment: "You shall love the Lord your God with all your heart, with all your soul, and with all your might." This is actually a description, not a commandment, since love of God is not something we can summon by an effort of the will. It's something we arrive at, naturally, as the mind deepens and matures; and we come closer to it the more clearly we understand that what is most valuable in this human life of ours is the unnamable, the inconceivable. It is everything, and also nothing, because it is beyond our categories of thought. It includes its own opposite: both/and, neither/nor. In the words of our teacher Spinoza, it is that which, when discovered and attained, allows us to experience continuous, supreme, and never-ending happiness, whatever may happen to us.

The Kabbalists called God אֵין סוֹף (*eyn sōf*), "the infinite," "the unending," and that is accurate too, as far as it goes. But what about the finite, the ending? Isn't God there (i.e., here) too? Isn't God that (i.e., this) too? "The whole earth is full of His glory," the seraphim chanted to Isaiah. Do we need to transcend the here and now in order to understand what is most important? Is that desirable? Is it even possible?

"Where have you come from?" an ancient Chinese Zen Master asked a monk who was seeking his instruction. "From the Monastery of Spiritual Light," said the monk. The Master said, "In the daytime, we have sunlight; in the evening, we have lamplight. What is spiritual light?" The monk, baffled, was silent. The Master answered for him: "Sunlight. Lamplight."

There is nothing mystical about this. Wisdom is a mode of love because it's a mode of presence—that is, of attention. The questioned mind sees itself in the same way that it sees the world: with awe and with deep gratitude. And it expresses its wonder in the language of pure reason as clearly as in the language of ancient scripture. Listen to the words of our teacher Einstein: "The scientist's religious feeling takes the form of a rapturous amazement at the harmony of natural law, which reveals an intelligence of such superiority that, in comparison with it, the highest intelligence of human beings is an utterly insignificant reflection."

From awe there are just a few steps to humility, from humility to wisdom, and from wisdom to happiness. The Book of Proverbs isn't kidding when it says, "Happy is the man who finds wisdom." That's simply the way of it. Joseph understood this.

Pity

BUT SOMETIMES, STILL, amid all his good fortune, he felt consumed by pity for his father. He would see an image of the old man weeping for his lost son and feel a tug at his heart and a childish desire to comfort that image. "Don't worry, Father," he wanted to tell it. "I'm alive. I'm well." And then he would wake out of the trance and realize that he had fallen into a mental trap. All this pity—what good was it doing? It didn't benefit Jacob in the least, and it left Joseph feeling sad and wrung out with helplessness. So he was compounding his father's suffering with his own. He was suffering over Jacob's suffering—over his own *imagination* of Jacob's suffering, really—and to what purpose? It was absurd.

Pity couldn't possibly be an appropriate response, because it cut him off from his own life energy. It was just as obvious that he wouldn't be able to help his father for a long time, if ever, however dearly he wished to. Jacob would have to find a way to help himself, as we all do ultimately. But Joseph had to stop thinking of him in this way. For weeks he struggled to find a point of equilibrium.

Finally, he decided to devote part of his morning prayers to contemplating his father in all his imagined misery, without any desire that he should be happy or that he should change in any way. This was extremely difficult at first, and it made Joseph heartsick. Then, over the months, it gradually became easier. Finally, he was able to see the image of Jacob's grieving face without any sense of pity or sorrow, but with a deep compassion that left his own heart at peace.

⬦

A Brief Chapter of Transition

ELEVEN YEARS PASSED. Joseph's good fortune came to extend over Potiphar's whole household and over everything he owned: the palace, the country house, the fields, the flocks and herds, the ships, the thoroughbred horses, the brewery, the copper mine, the in-house bank, and the in-house factory, a comfortable, pleasantly decorated building where female slaves spun flax into thread and wove linen garments.

Eventually Potiphar left all his affairs in Joseph's hands, so confident was he of the young man's extraordinary abilities.

Better Not

THE LAST OF THE WEEK'S GRAIN has been locked in the storehouse, the last numbers tabulated, the staff given their weekly message of encouragement and appreciation. Potiphar is out playing cards. (When he comes home, past midnight, drunk, gold clinking in his pockets, Joseph will undress him and tuck him into bed.) It is all working out smoothly, for now. The household is in perfect order. The profits accrue by themselves.

Joseph leans back in his adjustable chair and puts his feet up on the mahogany desk that was last year's birthday present from his boss. Was the story really going to end here, in loyalty, comfort, and superior accounting? He is fond of Potiphar, a sweet man, really, a cream puff of a man, for whom he wishes nothing but the best. But he knows God's ways. He had better not get too comfortable. He had better not lean back too far.

Potiphar's Wife

WE DON'T KNOW HER NAME. It has vanished from history (if it ever belonged there) and then from legend, until she stands beyond names now, in what William Blake might have called an incandescence of ungratified desire.

She was still a young woman, just three years older than Joseph. She had a passion for the beautiful, which manifested itself everywhere in her life. Her clothing and jewelry were supremely elegant, and her art collection was famous for its refinement. How could she not appreciate the young Hebrew slave, with his brilliant dark-brown eyes, his exquisite features, and his shapely body?

Over recent months, her interest in him had shifted from an intrigued noticing to a fascination and finally to an all-consuming obsession. Now she could barely take her eyes off him when occasionally he served in the role of butler and directed the footmen at a dinner party, and only the realization that her stares were rude and self-compromising could force her to look down at her plate or turn to one of her dinner companions.

She thought of him day and night. She wanted to resist the images, but they kept arising in her mind unbidden. She tried to talk herself out of this infatuation. The young man was a wretched slave, after all. He came from some obscure, unclean race. Yes, he was clever and highly esteemed by her lord husband, but undoubtedly he must be a fellow of low tastes and a coarse sensibility, however modest his outward demeanor might be—someone who could never appreciate the finer things that were her lifeblood, someone who in an intimate situation would no doubt disgust her as soon as he opened his charming lips.

But her reasons lacked conviction, and before long the images in her mind shifted to the sexual, the graphic. She was horrified at first. She tried to shut them out, but they kept appearing, then proliferating. Finally, her resistance snapped. She gave herself over to these images like someone who has been starving herself slim and suddenly breaks down and stuffs her mouth in the pantry. She even began to take the initiative, consciously elaborating the images into fantasies that made her quiver with lust and humiliation.

The more she indulged her obsession, the more her misery grew. Where would it end? How could she bear the disgrace if she did what she burned to do? But how could she endure in this wretchedness if she did nothing?

◇

Temptation

TEMPTED? OF COURSE HE IS TEMPTED—a flash of thigh through the sheer linen, her tongue slowly curling over her full lips, the beautiful long-lashed eyes meeting his and lingering, until he has to turn away. Or afternoons in the shadowed corridors, with no one nearby, a half-whispered *Fuck me oh please fuck me.* But never does he succumb, even as he waits for sleep, when her lithe image glides through his mind, stopping at the threshold of desire, wide-open-lipped, moist with longing. It isn't a matter of right and wrong, but of his own heart's wholeness, the truth he is in love with. Nor can he take on the role of hero, the splendid pattern of chastity, God's good boy, and allow himself the indulgence of not imagining her distress. He imagines it every day. But until a clear response is forced upon him, his duty is to keep walking the ever-narrower path between yes and no, the tightrope where one false step means (apparent) disaster.

A Clear No

FINALLY, ONE AFTERNOON, SHE GRABBED his arm and tried to pull him close, and he had no choice. "Please, madam," he said, "my master has entrusted me with everything in his estate and has held nothing back from me but you. You are very beautiful, and I am deeply honored by your attention. But I have to refuse."

Day after day she spoke to him, but there was no possibility that he would consent. His loyalty to his master was unshakable; he would as soon have cut off his own arm as betray him. Yes, his master's wife was a sexually alluring woman. But right away he had seen where that path led, and he had, like a sorcerer, drawn a magic circle around her in his mind, a circle she didn't have the power to step out of. And though he saw how miserable she was, and though he felt compassion for her, he knew that whatever she was longing for—intimacy? fulfillment?—was not in his power to give, even if he were to yield to the daily, mortified pleas and the helpless sobbing she broke into as he walked out of her presence with slow backward steps, his heart aching for her pain.

"Rape!"

ONE DAY, WITH HORROR, SHE REALIZED that the slave would never consent. There would be an infinite series of pleas and rejections, and she would keep sinking deeper and deeper into her despair. Her stomach turned in disgust at how pitiful she had become. Why couldn't he understand that and offer her at least a little sympathy? He had no idea of her loneliness or of the humiliation she was suffering, this pampered young man who had been given everything: good looks, good luck, the confidence of his master, the admiration of everyone in the palace. Why shouldn't *he* suffer too?

And how dared he resist her command? Who was he to resist? A slave, a barbarian! He was probably lusting for her anyway, secretly, and these arrogant scruples he purported to feel were just masks for his overweening ambition. He wanted her as much as she wanted him—even more, undoubtedly. And if she refused, the filthy little slave would take her by force. She was sure of it.

The next time he came in to do his work, she grabbed his

cloak and said, "Fuck me! Now!" But he got away, leaving the cloak in her hand, and hurried out of the room.

She screamed for her personal attendants. "Rape! Rape!" She was overwrought at first, almost inarticulate with rage and malice. After she calmed down, she said, "It was the Hebrew slave. He tried to rape me, but I screamed, so he ran out of the room, leaving his cloak behind."

When her husband came home, she said to him, "That Hebrew slave you've been pampering—he tried to rape me, but I screamed, and he ran out. Here is the cloak he left behind."

The Story Unravels

AT FIRST, POTIPHAR WAS INCENSED and deeply disappointed. But after she left the room, her story began to unravel in his mind. She was an accomplished actress, even when she was hysterical, as he knew from ten years of experience. And there was something about her account that didn't ring true. The glint of calculation in her eyes?

When he grew calmer and reflected on it, the whole story lost its coherence. Why would Meri-Amun risk his life for a few moments of pleasure, if pleasure is what that violent act would provide? The young man knew very well that slaves guilty of insubordination would be whipped and eviscerated and that the penalty for rape was even more gruesome: your body tied to a post, your genitals smeared with goat blood, a starving dog let loose to devour them—and that was just the first phase of the punishment, if you managed to survive.

Besides, Potiphar couldn't believe that he had been so radically mistaken about his protégé's character. True, the young man might suddenly have taken leave of his senses. But it was much more likely that the craziness issued from Potiphar's high-strung wife, who in moments of frenzy had been known to fling the most shocking accusations at her husband. Was he really going to summon Meri-Amun to defend himself? And then what? If he did defend himself, speaking with his usual eloquence, wouldn't his testimony expose the woman to humiliation before her servants, and wouldn't word of it get out? There were women at court, and men also, who would be only too pleased to circulate such a juicy tidbit of gossip. She would hate being talked about that way, and Potiphar would hate it just as much.

No, there could be no inquiry. The best way to proceed would be to take the young man into custody for a while. There was a prison on Potiphar's grounds (a privilege granted only to the highest court officials). It was a small, sand-colored brick building with two wings and three dozen cells, and he assigned Joseph to the wing reserved for prisoners of the crown. Potiphar would not, of course, be able to communicate with him. But he would make sure that he had all the amenities, a supply of books, and the goodwill of the warden.

As for the crime, if crime there had been, he couldn't bear to interrogate the young man or even to see him one last time. Who knew what his testimony would reveal?

Suddenly a wave of sorrow broke over his heart. Meri-Amun was gone—his dear, brilliant, beautiful Meri-Amun. What must he do now? Curtail his pleasures, to begin with; then take over the management of the estate, if he still had the ability and if the gods granted him the requisite strength of heart; or else find someone to replace Meri-Amun (as if there were anyone in the world who could).

The Insubstantiality of *Should*

JOSEPH WAS SURPRISED TO BE in prison, but not entirely surprised. He had been expecting some kind of upheaval, since the story couldn't end here, with such meager dimensions, and now, in his cell—it was actually a rather large and comfortable room, with a cot, a washbowl and pitcher, a desk, a window, and enough room for him to walk back and forth in contemplation—he had plenty of time to consider the turn of events, since the amiable warden had not yet assigned him any tasks.

When he looked back at his former situation in Potiphar's household, he realized how precarious it had become. For a long time he had felt a perfect balance in his life. There were no personal relationships to distract him, and he didn't need any. He had deepened his equanimity, grown stronger in his realization, and dedicated himself so entirely to excellence in his work that it felt like dedication to God. He was twenty-eight now, and during his eleven years in Potiphar's service, his skills as a manager, which had begun at a high level, had continued to improve. His master couldn't have been more pleased with his performance, and there had been no grumbling among the servants; indeed, he was universally admired for his rectitude and fairness. The morale was as high as it could be, and Potiphar often conveyed to him the heartfelt gratitude of the entire staff.

The only problem had been his master's wife. But that problem had lasted for months now, and it had turned out to be insoluble. Had Kedar been right when he said that all trouble comes from women? But that couldn't be true. The trouble in his father's life had begun in the womb, with the rivalry between him and his twin, Esau, and had continued through the duplicity of Laban, his father-in-law, as Joseph had heard many times in Jacob's after-dinner musings. And in Joseph's own life, it was obvious that the trouble that drove him to Egypt had had nothing to do with a woman; it had been caused by his brothers' hatred, which itself had been caused by his own arrogance and insensitivity.

He asked himself what similarities there might be between the two situations, then and now. Had he ever been arrogant toward his master's wife? Had there ever been anything inappropriate in his words or his bearing—anything that would make her feel looked upon as a sexually available woman rather than as the esteemed wife of his master? He tried to remember any breach of decorum in his bearing toward her, or even in his thoughts about her, but he could find no examples. Even after she had confessed her desire, he could find no negative judgment in himself, no lack of human sympathy.

If there was anything he could have done differently, it had to be in his relations with Potiphar. Perhaps he should have told him about the lewd overtures his wife had made. This thought had arisen once or twice at the time, but he had considered such a step premature. He had wanted to protect his master from an embarrassment that neither of them might know how to deal with. Even so, he should have told him. He should have been forthright.

But when he meditated more deeply on the subject, he realized that what he "should" have done was just a thought he was superimposing onto reality—or, more accurately, onto a past that now existed only in his imagination. How could he know what he should or shouldn't have done? How could he know that the best he could possibly have done was any different from what he had done in fact? And when he considered the whole course of events, how could he judge which was better: the unstable position he had been thrust from, in which he would continue indefinitely as Potiphar's majordomo, with his master's wife indefinitely pining away for him (for her imagined "him") and himself unwilling, unable, to assuage her desire; or the present transition, which would lead to who knew what? It would be presumptuous to think of the event as some kind of misstep or backward movement or fall from grace. Who could know the shape of the drama that had cast him as a prisoner for the time being? All he could be certain of was that everything had unfolded in accordance with the will of an intelligence so vast that in comparison his own was nothing—was less than nothing.

Dreams, Again

THREE MONTHS LATER, PHARAOH got angry at two of his ministers, the chief butler and the chief baker, and he put them under detention in Potiphar's prison. The chief butler, because of his access to Pharaoh, was a rich and powerful official; his position was a highly sensitive one, and his trustworthiness had to be impeccable, since there was an ever-present danger of bribery or mischief. The chief baker also ranked high on the list of palace officials, responsible as he was for some of the food that went directly into his sovereign's mouth.

Potiphar assigned Joseph to them as their attendant. His job was to visit them every morning and see that their needs were being met. He was also free to chat with them if he wished.

One morning he noticed that they were upset. "Gentlemen," he said, "you look out of sorts, both of you. What happened?"

"We had important dreams last night," the butler said, "but there is no expert here to interpret them."

Both men had had considerable experience with dream interpreters. Interpreting dreams was a popular occupation in Egypt, and at every level of society people consulted professionals. These ranged from the high priest of Amun—who, during court ceremonies, stood before Pharaoh in his elaborate regalia, alongside the most prominent court officials—down to the tawdriest psychics hawking their talents in the marketplace in front of wooden signs scrawled in simplified hieroglyphics with slogans that promised wealth and happiness to every client wise enough to linger. There were hundreds of dream books as well. Each one proposed a system that was, according to its creator, infallible. All you had to do in order to discover the correct meaning of any particular dream was to take every object in it, substitute the signified for the signifier on one of the long lists of equivalences, simplify the common elements among them as if you were factoring a quadratic equation, then fiddle with the spatial and temporal succession in one of the prescribed ways—and voilà, the meaning would appear before you, as obvious as a cracked egg. The most highly esteemed of these books claimed its descent from a prophet who, a thousand years before, had received his methodology from the god Ra himself, in his red-bodied, falcon-headed form, during a forty-day meditation retreat in the Theban desert. Copies of the book were rare and kept under lock and key. It took many years to master its dream grammar, but once you did and were certified by the proper authorities, you were assured of a position either at Pharaoh's court or at the court of one of the many princelings on the periphery of the empire, who were as de-

pendent on Egyptian superstitions as on the strength of the
Egyptian army.

"True interpretations come from God," Joseph said to
the butler. "Why don't you tell me your dream? I can interpret it."

He was supremely confident. He didn't consider himself a
prophet, a man through whose mouth God spoke. (The very
concept would have seemed ludicrous to him.) What he meant
by "True interpretations come from God" was that once you
let go of systems and methods of interpretation, and even of
the desire to interpret, the dream would interpret itself.

He had mused about this a great deal during his eleven
years in Egypt. Dreams, he had concluded, were simply uninhibited thinking. They presented you with what you knew
already but hadn't had the presence to be aware of. At their
best, when they weren't entirely the random or mischievous
play of the mind, they subtracted the habitual and left you with
essence: what your life would look like if you stepped beyond
personal interest and saw all things as forms of God, in an
ever-mutating, never-circumscribed flow. Dreams were, or
could be, prophetic of the future only because they illuminated
the present. It did not, after all, require prophetic powers to
see that a seed would become a stalk or a lamb a sheep.

He had often thought of those boyhood dreams that had
been the spark to the powder keg of his brothers' hatred. There
was an arrogance to them, as he was well aware. But in another sense they weren't about him at all, the person Joseph.
What his brothers, and his father as well, and his sweet dead
mother had been bowing down to was a quality that shone

through him like a flame through glass—an intelligence, a discernment, which could be called "the clear heart" as accurately as "the clear mind" and which he himself bowed down to in all humility. It wasn't him; it wasn't ever his. But if anything in the world could be called holy, that quality could.

The Butler's Dream

"IN MY DREAM," THE CHIEF BUTLER SAID, "I saw a vine in front of me. There were three branches on the vine, and as soon as it budded it blossomed, and its clusters ripened into grapes. Pharaoh's cup was in my hand, and I picked the grapes and squeezed them into the cup and handed it to Pharaoh."

It was easy for Joseph to equate the three branches with three days. Everyone knew that Pharaoh's birthday was coming soon, and it was the custom for him to deliver his judgments on that day: a list of honors and a list of punishments, recited by the stentorian voice of the high chamberlain amid the clucks and murmurs of the noble crowd. Nor was Joseph puzzled at the dream's tone. It was a dream of confidence and devotion, and although the butler had been upset, he spoke firmly now, with a smile, as he described how he had pressed the grapes and handed the cup to his master.

The butler was a short, plump man, with a shaved head, like all the nobility and priesthood, and luxuriant dark-brown eyebrows. Joseph could see that he was devastated by the

accusation of impropriety. It was obvious too that he wanted
nothing more than to clear his name. Whatever ambition or
venality might be lurking beneath the surface of his thoughts,
he was a loyal servant of Pharaoh, and it was a good bet, if not
a certainty, that at the birthday festivities his merits would
be recognized and he would be pardoned. It all depended on
his master. From everything Joseph had heard from Potiphar,
Pharaoh was an excellent judge of character, and you could depend on his good sense.

"This is what your dream means," Joseph said. "The three
branches are three days. Within three days, Pharaoh will summon you and restore you to your position, and you will be
handing Pharaoh his cup, just as you did before. So set your
mind at ease. And when your life has returned to normal, sir,
please do me a favor: speak about me to Pharaoh and ask him
to release me from prison. I have done nothing to deserve this
punishment."

The Baker's Dream

THE CHIEF BAKER, WHO HAD BEEN listening carefully, said to Joseph, "My dream was just like that. I saw three wicker baskets on my head. In the top basket there were all kinds of baked goods for Pharaoh, and birds were flying down and eating them."

He uttered the words in a bass monotone. He was a thin, louche-looking man whose eyes darted up, down, and around, without holding your gaze. Joseph noticed that in the dream there was no contact with Pharaoh. And why, except for guilt, with dozens of servants at his disposal, would the lord chief baker dream himself into a menial position, a mere transporter of baskets, the lowest rank in the kitchen? Why would the breads and cakes not make their way to Pharaoh, but be eaten up by birds before they could get to him? The baskets were obviously days, but what did the baked goods symbolize? Human flesh? And what about the birds? Could they be simply birds?

The baker's gloom filled the air.

Joseph could see no way to be tactful. "This is what your dream means," he said, looking directly into the baker's eyes. "The three baskets are three days. Within three days, Pharaoh will summon you and have you hanged, and birds will pick the flesh from your bones."

The baker was furious. He wanted to argue. But as he looked into Joseph's eyes, he realized that there was no arguing with the truth. He was a dead man.

A Broken Promise

THREE DAYS LATER, on his birthday, Pharaoh gave a feast for the high nobility, and he summoned the chief butler and the chief baker. He restored the chief butler to his former position, forgiving his peccadillo and welcoming him back with great warmth, and he had the chief baker hanged, just as Joseph had foretold.

Though the butler had fully intended to keep his promise, he gave no further thought to Joseph. He had been grateful to the handsome young barbarian for easing his mind during the last three days of the horrible captivity, and he would have been glad to do something for him. But the exhilaration of being back in Pharaoh's good graces, the joy of returning home to his wife and children and to the pleasures of court life, the feasts, the elaborate ceremonies in which his own movements were choreographed down to the minutest details, the horse racing, the hunting, the masques and musical entertainments, the flirtations with young women who were witty or pretty or both, the palace intrigues, the latest gossip about who was in and who was out—all this drowned out his promise like the din of a large crowd.

In fact, he did everything he could to avoid revisiting those months he had spent in prison under the heavy weight of his master's displeasure. It was too painful, and why should he purposely invite pain into his mind, now that he was back in the full current of life? Whenever a fleeting image of those months did appear, the young barbarian wasn't in it. All the butler could see was the bare cell with its wretched cot and himself pacing back and forth like a caged beast.

In Prison

TWO MORE YEARS WENT BY. At first Joseph hoped, though he knew better. Then he set hope aside, like a tool that has served its purpose and is no longer needed.

He didn't suffer at all during these two years. On the contrary, he enjoyed the simplicity of prison life. He needed nothing more than a desk and books and the sunlight that streamed through the cell's one window. Prison food was plain but hearty—bread, cheese, eggs, fish or fowl twice a week, sautéed vegetables, a mug of beer. And since the warden trusted him, he was allowed to move about freely, supervising projects, keeping the prison accounts, studying the Egyptian classics, and occasionally reading aloud to the soldiers on the prison staff from one of the famous manuals of moral instruction or from the great temple hymns, which in their exalted sense of the divine sometimes echoed his great-grandfather's sense of God. His favorite manual was *The Maxims of Ptahhotep*, with its clear, sensitive, practical advice: "Live in peace with what you have, and whatever else the gods give you will come on its own." "If the one who listens listens fully, he becomes the one who understands." And this one, which turned out to be prophetic for Joseph: "A woman with a happy heart brings happiness to all around her." He would recite these passages to the soldiers, one maxim at a time, and allow his audience five minutes of silence to find specific examples in their lives of where the maxim was, or might be, true. For some of the men, this exercise was illuminating.

Once a week the warden would invite him to his office for a couple of beers and a game of what we might call chess. The talk was very personal on the warden's part. He told Joseph about his wife, who was ill with some kind of women's disease, about the two sons he was so proud of, who were doing well in their studies for the civil service exams, and about the many problems and frustrations of his job. Joseph was reticent but convivial. Since he was a good listener, it always seemed that he contributed equally to the conversations. And though Joseph invariably won the game, the warden would pat him on the back afterward and say how refreshed he felt from their time together.

One day flowed into the next. It was all very pleasant, but Joseph knew that it was just an interlude. God, in His infinitely subtle wisdom, was pausing. He was thinking about His next move. He was holding Joseph between two fingertips as He scanned the squares of the world.

IV.
Viceroy of All Egypt

$\diamond$

Pharaoh's Dreams

THE IMPERIAL PRIVATE BEDROOM was decorated in yellow and blue, Pharaoh's favorite colors, emblems of sun and sky. He had decided to sleep alone tonight, giving himself a respite from the sexual needs of his nine wives and three concubines. He walked onto the terrace and stood there for ten minutes, leaning on the marble balcony, looking out over the vast expanse of the Nile, which lay before him glittering in the moonlight. Then he walked back into the room, picked up a corner of the blue-and-yellow duvet, and climbed into bed. It was early. He was very tired. The guards outside the door were under strict instructions to let no one in, however urgent the request might be.

He was a tall, vigorous man in his early forties—a good general, an efficient lawgiver, and a skilled manager, who had little patience for the inessential. He seldom remembered a dream, and when he did, he dismissed it with a smile, as you might dismiss a child who has been caught in a piece of inconsequential mischief.

But this dream was different. He had never before dreamed about the Nile, from which all blessings flow, and here he was, standing on its bank alone, with no courtiers around him, looking out not contemplatively but in expectation. And as if feeling had immediately become flesh, a cow poked her head from beneath the surface of the waters and ambled out onto the shore. She was plump and beautiful, her coat a dark reddish brown. As she stood in the sunlight with the water dripping from her flanks, another cow surfaced, walked out of the river, and stood beside her, and then another—seven in all, all of them healthy, plump, beautiful creatures, who stood there contentedly, facing away from the Nile as the water dripped from their flanks in the sunlight. Pharaoh looked on in amazement.

But now there was a sense of foreboding, and again feeling became flesh, and as he looked at the great river, seven more cows emerged from beneath the surface, one after the other— but these animals were emaciated and repulsive to look at. They moved toward the seven plump cows and then, to his horror, they devoured them, sucking them in from the tails until there was nothing left but the reddish-brown muzzles sticking out from their distended mouths, and then the muzzles too were sucked in, and everything about them was gone, and the seven gaunt cows looked as emaciated as before. At this point Pharaoh shuddered. He didn't know whether it was his body standing beside the Nile that shuddered or his body waking up in bed.

He tried to get back to sleep, but the sense of foreboding tossed and twisted his body from one position to another. When he finally fell asleep again, he had a second dream.

Seven healthy ears of grain, full and ripe and golden-yellow, were growing on one stalk. Then seven other ears, thin, dry, and shriveled by the east wind, sprouted close behind them. And the second stalk bent over toward the first stalk, and the thin, dry ears swallowed the full, healthy ears.

He woke up again, in a sweat.

Indecipherable

THE DREAMS HAD A SENSE OF urgency encoded in them, though it wasn't clear who or what was calling for a response. Pharaoh knew he had to act quickly. But how? What was he supposed to do, when the meaning of the dreams was indecipherable, like words written in an unknown script?

He hated uncertainty. As he walked from one end of his bedroom to the other and back again, hours before sunrise, his mind couldn't find a resting place, and his agitation grew. Like his revered ancestors, he had been entrusted by the gods with the welfare of the whole land, which depended on him the way a young child depends on its father and mother. It was his sound judgment and planning that secured the blessings of prosperity for every subject in his realm, from nobleman to peasant. Yet how could he even begin to assess the situation in his present state of confusion?

He felt as if his arms had been wrapped tight and bound to his torso by thick coils of rope from which he couldn't burst free. He wanted to pick up one of his priceless ancient vases and hurl it against the wall. He wanted to strangle someone.

The Dream Interpreters Deliver
Their Conclusions

ELEVEN IN THE MORNING. After a two-hour recess to consult the necessary lists and charts, the dream interpreters stood again before Pharaoh in their white pleated robes, holding their ebony staffs before them. One by one they delivered their conclusions.

The first interpreter said that the seven plump cows were seven powerful kings who would be utterly destroyed by the leanest of forces from Pharaoh's invincible army; the seven ripe ears were seven potential diseases that would be obliterated by the ministrations of Pharaoh's skilled and faithful physicians, whose thinness signified their constant concern for their master's welfare. The second interpreter said that the seven plump cows were seven foreign princesses who would be sent as brides to Pharaoh with offers of alliance, and the lean cows were the resulting children who would suck at their mothers' breasts. And so on.

Each interpretation was delivered with absolute confidence. After the last one, the assembled sages announced through their foreman that whichever particular interpretation Pharaoh in his wisdom should be pleased to decide on, the purport of his dreams was absolutely clear: that heaven's grace would shine on His Serene Majesty now and forever, and that the future could only bring him still more of that glory which he enjoyed at present and which he was destined to enjoy for eternities to come.

Pharaoh shook his head in disgust. All the interpretations were mere flattery and formulaic nonsense. What did they have to do with the dread he had woken up with?

Then the chief butler remembered. It returned to him in a flash: the young barbarian, the prediction, the release, the exhilaration of being back in his master's good graces. He was deeply ashamed that he had broken his word. There was no remedy for it but to lay the whole story before Pharaoh. The young man deserved at least that.

As soon as the butler had finished speaking, Pharaoh ordered that Joseph be summoned from prison.

The Summons

THE PAPYRUS SCROLL WAS TIED with a golden ribbon and sealed in purple wax with the imperial scarab. The warden brought it to Joseph, then discreetly withdrew. (He also left a fresh white robe of the highest-quality linen and a pair of expensive sandals.)

Joseph opened the scroll. The message was written in the hieratic script, with black and red ink. He was to appear before Pharaoh in two hours.

Ah. So the chief butler had mentioned him at last.

The summons must have something to do with dreams; that is what the butler would have reported. Pharaoh must have had an important dream, and Joseph was being called on to interpret it. He didn't know how he would do this, but he knew that he could.

He lathered his face and skull,* stropped his razor, and

---

* Rabbi Hananiyah the Miller said, "Joseph looked just like an Egyptian. As it is said, 'On every head there is baldness, and every beard has been shaved.'" (Isa. 15:2) Rabbi Abtalion bar Nuri of Carmel said, "If we are to stand out from the Gentiles, let it be by our inward spirit. As it is said, 'A man's wisdom makes his face shine.'" (Eccles. 8:1)

looked into the small chipped mirror that hung above the washbasin. The eyes that looked back at him shone with excitement.

But beneath the excitement, he could feel a deep calm. *Don't expect Pharaoh to acknowledge you.* As the thought surfaced into consciousness, he smiled. Was it a warning? A superstitious charm against disappointment? Or was it itself a recognition of the futility of trying to force the present into one of a trillion possible futures, none of which can be judged in advance?

The razor glided down his cheek, and he could feel the momentary resistance of the stubble, then the letting go. Where the blade had cut a swath through the white lather, the skin was as smooth as a baby's.

"Not I"

CROWDS OF COURTIERS PARTED to let Joseph and the two guards walk through the throne room. Now he stood right before the steps that led up to Pharaoh's throne. The throne was overlaid with gold and adorned with semiprecious stones. Its two lion's-head finials stared threateningly at Joseph, as if they were about to let out two miniature roars.

"I had a dream," Pharaoh said, in a voice booming with authority, "but no one can discover its meaning. I have heard about you. I am told that you know how to interpret dreams."

"Not I," Joseph said. "Not I but God will give Pharaoh the correct interpretation."

What god was the young barbarian referring to? Pharaoh examined him carefully. He tried to read his face. He could see no signs of trickery in it, but he could find no wisdom either. The face was impenetrable. Was it just that the young man's beauty deflected any deeper probing into the character that lay beneath it?

Joseph's confidence was not in himself—or rather, it was

not in any self that he could identify. It was in what remained when he stepped aside from the self he knew as Joseph. In that state of inner alertness, he became the listener, with no intentions, no preconceptions, no opinions to defend, no outcome to wish for. The still, small voice that arose inside him was the voice of God, but it was also the voice of reason, stripped of the ordinary selfish distortions that desire and aversion impose. It existed beyond the concepts of good and bad, fortune and misfortune, since God was beyond all opposites, and His presence was infused through the world so intimately that Joseph couldn't help hearing the word *misfortune* as a failure of insight. A misfortune is a blessing that has not yet been recognized. In Joseph's experience there was only God's blessing, and behind its sometimes fearsome disguises it was always waiting to be discovered. Whatever apparent misfortune these dreams might foreshadow could be turned to the benefit of all, if only Pharaoh would pay attention.

◇

Just One Meaning

PHARAOH TOLD JOSEPH HIS TWO DREAMS in as much detail as he could remember. "I described all this to my dream interpreters," he concluded, "but none of them could come up with a meaning that made any sense."

The remarkable thing about Egyptian dreams was not that they might be direct revelations of God—Joseph could see no reason to be proprietary about revelations, since, for all he knew, God was just as concerned about the welfare of the Egyptians, the Mesopotamians, and the Canaanites as He was with the welfare of Joseph's own tribe—but that the dreams hypostatized time as space. Three branches; three baskets. The threes had been easy to equate with days, since back then Pharaoh's birthday lists had been on everyone's mind. And the sevens: could they too be days? No, in the context of cattle and grain, good and bad seasons, they had to symbolize years. So: good years and bad years, one series after the other, years of abundance and years of deprivation, abundance eaten up by deprivation.

This conclusion was not reasoned out. It simply appeared to him, all at once, outside the confines of temporal succession. If it occurred in time, the reasoning had been compressed into a fraction of a second, inside which Joseph felt he had all the time in the world, just as a great athlete at the peak of his game can enter a mental zone in which a second expands to contain minutes, and a tennis ball, for example, hurtling forward at a hundred miles an hour, seems as if it is floating lazily over the net, fat as a melon.

"Pharaoh's dreams can have just one meaning," Joseph said. "God has told Pharaoh what He is about to do. The seven healthy cows are seven years, and the seven healthy ears of corn are the same seven years; the seven lean cows that followed behind them are the seven years that will follow, and so are the seven shriveled ears—they are seven years of famine. Seven years of great abundance are coming to Egypt, but they will be followed by seven years of famine, and the famine will be so severe that nothing will be left of all the abundance, and death will consume the land. So Pharaoh should look for a man who has foresight and wisdom, and he should put this man in charge of all the affairs of Egypt. Pharaoh should also appoint supervisors to gather all the surplus grain that is harvested during these years of abundance, to collect it under Pharaoh's authority and bring it into the cities and store it there. That grain will be a reserve for the seven years of famine, and the people will be saved, and the land will not be destroyed."

Silence. All eyes turned toward Pharaoh. All ears waited for his words.

The Man

"PHARAOH SHOULD LOOK FOR A MAN"? Joseph hadn't planned on saying any such thing.

He was surprised as the words issued from his mouth, but as a listener he could feel the rightness of what he, as the speaker, was saying. It had been masterly, that leap from interpretation to suggestion, and it had been performed with such exquisite finesse that if anyone else had done it, Joseph would have clapped his hands in admiration. But it *had* been someone else; it *was* someone else; certainly, the self he was conscious of wasn't the self that had spoken those words, so forceful and at the same time so courteous that they had made the suggestion seem modest, as if the invisible flashing arrows that now pointed straight at him were not his creation at all but sprang from Pharaoh's own inspired insight.

However the idea had emerged, it was now a fact. He himself was the man he had suggested. He knew it, and everyone else in the room did too. It was clear to him now that he had been chosen for this job since the day of his birth—since the beginning of time. At this moment he had only a dim sense of what he would need to know or do to accomplish the great task. But he was certain that the details would reveal themselves to him as he proceeded. The solution had to be already present in the problem, as the meaning had been present in the dream.

In Charge

PHARAOH WAS DELIGHTED WITH THE PLAN.* He turned to his ministers and said, "How could we find anyone equal to this man, who is filled with the spirit of the gods?"

His rhetorical question had nothing to do with gods. He was not looking for inspiration, and he didn't give a damn where Joseph's brilliance came from. What he meant by "the spirit of the gods" was the spirit of practical wisdom, especially in political economy and statesmanship. Since he too knew how to listen to the still, small voice, on the rare occasions when it whispered to him, he had needed just a moment to perceive the young man's outstanding ability, and he trusted this perception enough to bet the well-being of his whole empire on it.

"There is no one," he said to Joseph, "with such foresight and wisdom as you. Therefore, I am putting you in charge of

---

* Rabbi Hanina bar Yonatan of Jenin said, "Being a man of discernment, Pharaoh could recognize that Joseph was a truth-teller. As it is said, 'Righteous lips are a wise king's delight.'" (Prov. 16:13)

all Egypt, and all my people will obey your commands. Only in court matters will my authority be greater than yours."

He took off his gold signet ring, which would enable Joseph to sign legal documents in Pharaoh's name, and put it on Joseph's finger, and he gave him a ceremonial robe of the finest white linen and a thick gold chain of office to put on. Joseph looked particularly handsome in this robe, with the gold chain of office around his neck.

God's Little Joke

JOSEPH ACCEPTED THE POSITION as viceroy with appropriate grace, but inwardly he was wary, since he understood how easily wealth and power can corrode a man's integrity, in gross or barely perceptible ways. He would have to be extremely careful not to confuse his own personal will, empowered now to the utmost degree, with the will of the supreme intelligence.

But he enjoyed his privileges. All the pomp and circumstance was amusing, actually, and he had to smile at God's humor in having these slim young heralds with pomaded hair run ahead of his chariot crying, "Bow down! Bow down!" while the surging crowds obeyed, echoing and magnifying his dreams of thirteen years before, though only he and God could appreciate the joke.

Asenath

SO PHARAOH MADE JOSEPH RULER over all Egypt, and he be-
stowed on him the name Zaphnath-paneakh, which means
Through Him the Living God Speaks. The imperial proclamation read as follows:

> To my subjects, the people of the Black Land: I hereby
> command that you obey Zaphnath-paneakh, my newly
> appointed viceroy, as if he were myself, thinking with
> my mind and speaking with my tongue. From this mo-
> ment forth, no one shall undertake or continue any
> project anywhere in Egypt or throughout the lands of
> my empire without my viceroy Zaphnath-paneakh's
> written approval.

Pharaoh also married Joseph to Asenath, daughter of Potiphera, the high priest of Ra in the city of Ōn.

During Joseph's moony romantic years, at fourteen or fifteen, he had imagined marrying within the tribe: a pretty

Jewish cousin or niece. But obviously God had other ideas for him. Asenath was as Gentile as they came: short straight nose, honey-blond hair, creamy rose-tinged skin, lips like ripe plums, blue eyes that shone with joy, and a supple, elegantly accommodating nature that was the opposite of the sometimes unpleasant willfulness of Joseph's great-grandmother Sarah or his grandmother Rebecca. (He knew them well through Jacob's stories.)

Pharaoh had presented Asenath to him as a paragon among women, "precious beyond all things," as the Book of Proverbs says, and Joseph fully realized her value and treasured her. He was monogamous by temperament. There were many temptations at the Egyptian court—women, that is, who might have tempted a man not entirely focused on the two things in the world that mattered to Joseph: his marriage and his work. Both these realms were the context for his reverence, the form that his worship of God took, since it was to them that he gave himself with all his heart. The dozens of women who shot him the unmistakable look of desire that he had seen in the eyes of Potiphar's wife barely made an impression. He knew how to glide past them with a few kind words, then move on to what was important.

Life with Asenath

THEIR HOUSE IN MEMPHIS was far too big, but Asenath had
grown up accustomed to such splendor, and Joseph wouldn't
have wanted her sense of abundance to be diminished in any
way, especially since the obverse of her generosity to herself
was her generosity to others. The house had been a gift from
Pharaoh on their wedding day. Actually, it was difficult to
think of it as a house; it was a palace, built of marble, limestone, and granite, and it had dozens of elegantly furnished
rooms in it, most of which he and Asenath didn't use except
for the weekly ceremonial dinners they gave for the high nobility, the leading government officials, and foreign diplomats.
The library was Joseph's favorite room. It housed a comfortable armchair, an elegant secretary desk and chair, and ceiling-
to-floor scroll cases stocked with the finest examples of
Egyptian and Akkadian poetry, philosophy, and political
economy.

The walls of the palace were painted a brilliant white on
the outside and rich colors on the inside. Glazed ceramic tiles

covered the surfaces, decorated with geometric patterns or images from nature: flowers, birds, grapevines, palm trees and cedars, red calves grazing in green meadows, green calves grazing in violet meadows. On the floor of the master bedroom, a famous craftsman had painted scenes of the Nile, teeming with fish of all varieties, its banks a flutter of egrets, pelicans, ibises, storks, geese, and ducks. Red, blue, and yellow S-shaped spirals and bull's heads covered its ceiling, which was supported by limestone columns in the form of giant lilies.

When he first moved in, Joseph had felt annoyed by all this luxury. It had seemed extravagant, a colossal waste of time and money, and an unnecessary, frivolous tug at his attention. But he realized that the luxury couldn't be avoided; it was the proper and visible sign of his stature as viceroy, and besides, it delighted Asenath. So he adjusted his mind to the new circumstances, and he quickly came to accept, and even enjoy, what God, in the guise of Pharaoh, had so generously presented him with.

Running the household and maintaining the building and grounds required a hundred servants: private secretaries, treasurers, a butler, valets, ladies-in-waiting, apothecaries, bakers, brewers, cooks, kitchen maids, gardeners, grooms, stable boys, house cleaners, and pages. Though Joseph found it easy to manage them, he would sometimes feel a subtle strain on his mind during the day, when the palace was swarming with bodies. He would maintain his equilibrium by shutting himself in his library for a few hours. On days like this he would long for evening to arrive, when the servants were gone and he could be alone with his beloved.

Asenath was beautiful, and people fell in love with her all

the time, both men and women. It wasn't her physical beauty they found so enchanting, though of course that played a part in their response. It was her happiness—her blessedness, you might even call it. It seemed to flow from her heart and fill her eyes with its luster. When you were in her presence, you felt included in this happiness; you felt you were sharing it somehow, as if there were an endless supply in her that was available to you for the taking. While she spoke with you, even if you were a scullery maid or a field slave, you felt that she held you in her gaze as if you were the only person on earth—as if, for those moments, you were the beloved. Joseph witnessed this often, and he loved her all the more for it.

She was extraordinary in many other ways. She had a high intelligence, as high as Joseph's, though it took an entirely different form. His was quick; hers was leisurely, and he sometimes had to call on his considerable reservoir of patience as he waited for her to settle on a decision, which, once it happened, was ironclad. Joseph's intelligence was direct: it moved in a straight line from point A to point B; Asenath's meandered like an ant, in wavering lines, forward, sideways, backward, diagonally, in circles and epicycles of circles, on its way from point A to point B or, bypassing B, to an unsuspected, astonishing point Z, in a movement that seemed random but had complex mathematical roots. Though Joseph's prayer life was a practice of listening, his natural mode was visual, at times visionary; Asenath heard things. Her thinking was like music: rhythmical, melodious, and self-consistent. Sometimes, in the midst of a thought, she would burst into peals of silvery laughter.

She was absolutely uninhibited about her emotions. When

she laughed or cried, it was an onslaught of the most intense delight or sorrow. If she got angry at him, as she sometimes did (usually for a good reason), the anger was pure, without malice or blame—a natural phenomenon, like a summer storm or a flash flood—and when it was spent, after five minutes or ten, it left no residue. She would look at him again with loving eyes, as if the emotion had flared up a thousand years ago, as if its momentary cause had been forever wiped from the face of the earth.

Her integrity was impeccable. She was the most honest human being Joseph had ever met. He could always trust that her yes was a yes and her no a no. There was no pretense or ulterior motive in them. She never spoke to gain his love or approval. She needed no one's love or approval but her sweet own, which was the underpinning of her spectacular generosity. Joseph experienced this with profound admiration. *I have married my equal*, he would think. *I have joined with my wife, like Adam in the Garden, and we have become one flesh.*

She had her own world of interests, a world of art, music, and devotion to the sun god Ra, and Joseph never felt that he needed to keep her amused. Her days were as full as his were, with matters that captivated her imagination, and when she and Joseph met in the evening, their focus was on each other.

She was a remarkable listener. Joseph too knew how to listen, but the quality of Asenath's listening went beyond anything he had ever known. When he began a serious conversation with her, it was as if he had stepped into an atmosphere of such purity that his mind deepened and expanded to meet it, the way breath deepens in the mountain air. He didn't dominate their conversations; there was a flow; she spoke almost as much as he did, and the loveliest games of wit and seduction spontaneously arose for their mutual delight. But when he spoke and she listened, he could hear himself think newly, differently, as if his idea had been transformed by the act of resonating through her silence, as if it had returned to his ears freed from the stubbornly male, the stubbornly Joseph— had returned to him as much hers as his, like a child who resembles both parents, each in a different way.

In-Laws

ASENATH'S FATHER, POTIPHERA (accent on the third syllable), is not to be confused with Potiphar (accent on the first syllable), captain of the guard, who, as you may remember, was incapable of having children. Potiphera was the high priest of Ra in Ōn (rhymes with *stone*), one of the most ancient cities in Egypt.

Joseph had no problem with becoming the son-in-law of a pagan priest. On the contrary, he was delighted that Pharaoh had wished him to marry into one of the old priestly families, the high aristocracy of the kingdom, because they—some of them—were the most educated and discerning of people. He had the greatest respect for Potiphera's devotion to a god who, as giver of life, was in many ways the same generous presence that Joseph himself revered. And this was not just talk; his father- and mother-in-law were among the most decent, honest, charming, disinterested, charitable people he had ever met.

He greatly enjoyed the periodic visits he and Asenath made

to his in-laws. Asenath's mother was a witty, cultured lady, who had at first been resistant to welcoming a barbarian into her illustrious family, however powerful or honored he might be. But the more she came to know Joseph, the more her judgments softened, until by the third visit she was treating him with as much affection and respect as Asenath could have wished for.

Potiphera had had no such prejudices. He had immediately recognized the quality of Joseph's mind, and their relationship had been warm and candid from the beginning. After dinner, when the ladies had retired to the drawing room, he and Joseph would sit together in two of the easy chairs that lined the colonnade, drinking the ancient Egyptian equivalent of vintage port and talking about the divine. Potiphera's intellect was too subtle to identify Ra with the physical sun alone, much less with the slender falcon-headed man whom the masses worshipped. He shared with Joseph a trust in an all-embracing providence. But he had difficulty with Joseph's reverence for what was unsayable and unknowable. He was, Joseph thought, too attached to the light to realize that it is also its opposite. In short, his concept of God was too narrow. But then, so was Joseph's. So was any human mind's.

In Joseph's capacity as viceroy, he was obligated to participate in certain state-sponsored religious ceremonies, and while much of the ritual and mythology, as well as the constant references to an afterlife, seemed trivial and foolish to him, there were moments when he could give the words of the liturgy his wholehearted assent, especially in the Great Hymn to the Sun, chanted in the House of Atum by a choir of two hundred young men and women. "You appear on the horizon," they sang, and Joseph would feel his flesh begin to tingle. He knew all the words that would follow, beautiful and true in themselves and tuned to a melody that curled its way up and down the Lydian scale in slow, willowy waves.

You appear on the horizon, glorious
    sun, begetter of life.
When you rise in the eastern sky,
    you fill the whole world with your beauty.
Though you are far away,
    you send your light to the earth;
though you shine on men's faces,
    your pathways cannot be seen.
You appear to us, and the darkness
    fades, and all beings rejoice,
and you shine out to the limits
    of everything that you made.
Men wake and stand on their feet;
    they wash and put on their clothing
and lift up their arms to thank you,
    then go out to do their work.
Cattle browse in the pastures,
    trees and grasses flourish,
geese flutter in the marshes
    and stretch out their wings to the sky
    in adoration of you,
sheep dance on their hooves,
birds fly into the air
    and rejoice that you shine upon them,

fish in the river leap up
before you, and your rays plunge
into the Great Green Sea.
Creator of the seed in women,
you care for the unborn child,
you soothe him so he won't cry,
you bring him into the air,
you open his mouth and give him
everything that he needs.
When the chick speaks through the eggshell,
you send him the breath of life
and bring his form to completion;
he pecks his way out and stands up
chirping with all his might.
How manifold is your creation,
O one and only God!
How beautiful is this world
created as your heart desired it
when you were all alone!
How beautiful is this world
with its billions of living creatures!—
whoever swims in the sea
or walks about on the earth
or flies through the heavens above it.

Potiphar Again, and His Wife

PHARAOH HAD ARRANGED FOR many dozens of introductions after the investiture ceremony, to princes and priests from all the ancient, still-powerful families, so that Joseph had only a few minutes with each person who approached his throne to bow or curtsy before him. Everyone wished him well, with the latest, chic-est variations on the courtly phrases they had been using since childhood, and after a while, in order to stave off his incipient boredom, it occasionally amused him to intercept one of these phrases on the wing and hand it back to the speaker with slightly ruffled feathers. Some of the noblemen and -women responded with blank stares; others looked panicked at first, then closed their eyes and bowed discreetly to end the conversation; a few laughed with pleasure at the new viceroy's wit. But when Joseph became aware of the discomfort he was causing, he stopped the repartee and settled back into his boredom as if into an overstuffed armchair.

After thirty minutes or so, Potiphar and his wife came up to present themselves. Potiphar was all smiles. He looked like a proud father on the day of his son's graduation. Congratulations and well-wishes sprang from his lips like the curlicues and flourishes of an antique signature, in language that was entirely conventional yet obviously sincere, since the sentiments were mirrored and confirmed on his beaming face. He had been discreet, he assured Joseph with a bow, about the reason for Joseph's imprisonment; his wife's slaves had been sworn to secrecy, on pain of torture; no one else knew, and no one ever *would* know. Joseph couldn't have cared less what people said about him behind his back, but he gave Potiphar a warm smile and a thank-you. Then he turned to her.

She looked stunning tonight, in a shimmery royal-blue sheath that fell from just below her breasts to just above her ankles and was held up by two broad royal-blue shoulder straps. Adorning her chest was a large pectoral made of gold, carnelian, lapis lazuli, ruby, quartz, and turquoise, depicting a blue falcon with gold-and-green wings. Her cheeks were flushed; it was obvious that she was feeling strong emotions, but Joseph couldn't tell what they were. After the herald announced her name, she made a deep curtsy to Joseph, keeping her eyes cast down on the ground.

He had thought about her often during his time in prison, and he had never blamed her. She had obviously been out of her mind when she had accused him of rape, unaware of the gruesome punishment she was condemning him to—or if she *had* been aware of it, that just proved how disordered her thinking had been. He knew how acutely she had been suffering and how trapped she had felt by her uncontrollable desire. It was easy to see how this desire had tipped over into hatred. The poor woman had been desperate. How could he blame her for that?

He watched her curtsy. He wondered if she was feeling any fear of reprisals, now that he had been granted such power. After she rose, he said to her, very gently, "I hope you are well, my lady. I wish you all the happiness in the world."

She nodded in acknowledgment but kept her eyes lowered. Then she and Potiphar stepped backward and away, as the next couple approached the throne.

Why Joseph Sent No News Home

"HOW COULD JOSEPH NOT HAVE had compassion on his agèd father?" asked the thirteenth-century philosopher, physician, and biblical commentator Moshe ben Nachman. "How could he not have sent even one letter home to let Jacob know that he was alive? Hebron is only a six-day journey from Egypt. Respect for his father would have justified a *year's* journey." The moral indignation that crackles through his words is beautiful, don't you think? Painful but beautiful. And when you consider the situation, it does at first seem like a grave offense for Joseph to have broken the Fifth Commandment so flagrantly, even though the Fifth Commandment didn't yet exist.

Here is the explanation.

Once Joseph had been made viceroy and was free to do whatever he wanted, not a day went by when he didn't think of sending a letter to Jacob or making the trip to Hebron himself. He imagined the homecoming in vivid detail: how he would arrive at Jacob's tent hardly able to contain his excitement, how he would step through the entrance and run to his astonished father and hold him in his arms. He could see it all, could smell his father's skin and feel the roughness of his beard against his cheek, with such a sense of reality that it made the present moment feel like a dream. For the first week or so, going home was a daily, almost irresistible temptation.

The more he prayed about it, though, the less right it seemed for him to do anything of the sort. This is how he prayed: First he pictured himself sending a letter home or actually going home. (He never saw his brothers in the image—only his grieving father.) Then he infused that image with a wordless question, and he waited, listening. The process was like the echolocation of a bat: casting sound waves against the walls of the cave to hear exactly where you're flying. The echo of his wordless question always returned to him as a no.

He was, as you can understand, very interested in that no. Everything moral, everything filial, decent, and humane, pointed to a yes. Why shouldn't he let his poor anguished father know that he was alive? What possible reason could there be to prolong the old man's grief, even for a day, even for a minute? And yet the no was clear and consistent. He had no doubts. He just didn't understand the why of it.

It probably had to do with his change of circumstance. If Jacob knew that he was alive, he would surely want him to return to Canaan and, just as surely, would refuse to leave the land where his father and grandfather were buried. This would be an insoluble problem, which would only cause the old man further, needless suffering, since Joseph couldn't possibly leave Egypt. He had been entrusted with the welfare of the whole country, and he had a thousand things to do, a thousand things to learn, during the seven years of abundance. Of course, in working for the good of the Egyptians, he was working for the good of his father as well. The need was urgent. If he didn't carry out his plan in the most meticulously thorough way, his father would starve, along with his brothers and their families and everyone else in Canaan. How could he move his focus away from that mission? So wasn't it better for his father to continue believing that he was dead—a thought he had undoubtedly become accustomed to—than to know that he was alive and unable to come home, a situation that would be incomprehensible to the old man and might even seem to him like defiance and be a fresh cause for grief?

The echoing no might also refer to his brothers. If they hadn't repented, his forgiveness would mean nothing to them. Forgiveness, he knew, didn't have to be deserved or earned, and in any case his forgiveness had already happened, unpremeditated; it was already there for them, whenever they could bear to receive it. But for it to be of benefit, the transaction had to be mutual. Without their awareness of wrongdoing, followed by their sincere remorse, there would be nothing he could do to help them, and he very much wanted to help them if he could. He felt a welling-up of love for these men, and it was easy to imagine what a heavy burden of conscience they might have been carrying all these years. He would have to find out if they had repented. How he could do this, he had no idea.

The truth was that he was waiting for a sign. Revealing himself to his family was his heart's desire, but the timing was crucial. He didn't yet know what to do, and he trusted that not-knowing. He refused to take any action that was motivated by his merely personal desire, however moral it might seem.

The action would have to happen spontaneously, without his conscious intervention—that is, it would have to be presented to him on a silver platter by the hand of providence. He was confident that he would be able to recognize it when it appeared.

Faith

I'D LIKE TO PAUSE HERE AND CONSIDER Joseph's trust in not-knowing. Though he'd had to discover it for himself, in the back of his mind was the example of his great-grandfather Abraham, who had discovered that faith has nothing to do with what we believe; it's the realization that what we can't know is wiser than all our knowing. This realization is a difficult one, because it destroys the illusion that we have control over our lives. It leaves us where we are in reality: between a past that couldn't have been other than what it was and a future of pure possibility, which can't ever be what we imagine. For someone who has seen beneath the surface of the chattering mind, this infinitesimal, instantaneously vanishing space between past and future becomes habitable; it becomes home. In its clarity, the whole world becomes clear.

There were things that Joseph did know. He never wavered from his certainty about the coming famine and the measures to counteract it, though the specific details were fuzzy at first and came into focus only as he approached them, learning as he went. He knew that he was capable of governing the land of Egypt. He knew, from the first moment he looked into her eyes, that Asenath was the love of his life. These realizations were immediate, vivid, and self-evident. Still, he subjected each of them to an unsparing examination. He wanted to be certain of his certainty, to test whether it was in any sense a convenience of the ego or a veneer that overlay hidden modes of arrogance or incapacity. He was a scientist of the mind and strictly observed what the physicist Richard Feynman called the first principle of science: "You must not fool yourself—and you are the easiest person to fool."

But experiences of knowing were as rare as they were incontrovertible. When he didn't know what to do, as with the question of revealing himself to his family, he respected that state of mind. He was at ease with the not-knowing, whether it lasted seven minutes or seven years, and he remained alert to any irritable reaching after a certainty that was based on his own desire rather than on reality. Any kind of premature or partial knowing would be a death, as if he had bitten into the fruit of the Tree of the Knowledge of Good and Evil, which stood in the Garden, beautiful and seductive, beside the Tree of Wisdom, also known as the Tree of Life.*

He would know what to do about his brothers when he needed to know it, and not a moment before. Providence was not something that descended from the heavens or was im-

---

* Rabbi Gershon ben Yehuda of Tiberias said, "The fruit of the two trees had opposite effects: knowing and unknowing. Knowing is the death of awareness; unknowing is eternal life. As it is said, 'He who increases knowledge increases sorrow' (Eccles. 1:18) and 'Wisdom is the tree of life for those who become intimate with her.'" (Prov. 3:18)

posed onto reality from the outside. Providence *was* reality. It was woven into the texture of everything that happened. That was why he could trust whatever happened, whenever it happened.

Famine

DURING THE SEVEN ABUNDANT YEARS, when the earth produced crops in a profusion that not even the oldest great-grandfathers and great-grandmothers had ever witnessed, Joseph traveled throughout Egypt and gathered all the surplus grain and brought it into the cities, and in each city he stored the grain that was grown in that area. He understood that physical blessings are always temporary and need to be supplemented by an intelligent economic policy, which can be administered only by a central government. In that sense, government too is a blessing from God. Without it, class inequalities would deepen, and the poor would languish. So he collected vast quantities of grain. Some of his awed deputies said that this grain was immeasurable, like the sands of the sea.

Before the years of famine arrived, two sons were born to him and Asenath. They divided the naming: Asenath chose the boys' names in Egyptian and Joseph in Hebrew. The two names she chose had been in her family for hundreds of years; both were variations on ancient temple phrases that gave thanks to Ra, the All-Radiant, the All-Compassionate. As for Joseph, he named the firstborn son Manasseh (He Who Causes to Forget), meaning "God has allowed me to forget myself," and the second son Ephraim (Fruitful), meaning "God has made me fruitful in my adopted land." Manasseh took after his esteemed, adorable mother, and Ephraim was in many ways a young version of himself. He loved them both, deeply, equally.

Then the seven years of abundance came to an end, and the seven years of famine began, just as he had foretold. There was no rain. The crops failed. Some of the palace elite, in private, began to parody the Great Hymn to the Sun: "You appear on the horizon, ominous / sun, begetter of death," they would chant with bitter irony, sotto voce.

When the people cried out for food, Pharaoh issued a brief proclamation:

To my subjects, the people of the Black Land: Go to my viceroy, Zaphnath-paneakh, during this famine. He is in charge of distributing the grain, as of everything else in our country, and he will feed you.

Joseph had his deputies open the storehouses and sell grain to the Egyptians. He didn't set one price for all people. For noblemen and rich landowners, he quadrupled the base price, then six months later he doubled it again. There were outraged murmurs, but Pharaoh had made it clear that resistance to Joseph was resistance to himself. Besides, the rich had no choice. Though they had known of Joseph's efforts, they hadn't been aware of any need to store grain for themselves, and like the prodigal grasshopper, they came empty-handed to Joseph, the provident ant. For the middle classes, Joseph kept the price reasonable—a strain, but not beyond what they could afford. To the poor, he gave grain free of charge. Any grumbling about the unfairness of this policy occurred behind closed doors in the homes of the rich and the well-to-do.

The famine grew worse, not only in Egypt but in all the neighboring countries. Those who could, sent envoys to Joseph; those who couldn't, died.

V.

Joseph Reveals Himself

◇

In Canaan

HOW MANY YEARS HAD IT BEEN since Joseph left his home in Canaan? Let's see. He was seventeen at the time, and he spent eleven years in Potiphar's service, two years in prison, then he was made viceroy. So that's thirteen, plus the seven years of abundance and, say, a year of famine, which makes a total of twenty-one. During those twenty-one years, Jacob was occasionally drawn out of his grief, but not for long. He was able to celebrate when his sons got married and had children of their own (the eleven sons had a total of twenty-five wives, and by now there were forty-nine grandsons and thirty-seven granddaughters). But it seemed to him as if it were someone else's family that was prospering. His pleasure, tepid at its warmest, seemed to be happening to someone else. He couldn't help thinking of Joseph even during the wedding ceremonies, wondering what kind of woman could possibly have been good enough for him or imagining the boy's beautiful face onto the children he would have had.

After Joseph disappeared, it took Jacob years to surface into life from the depths of the despair he had fallen into. The best times for him, the days when he was able to regain some small measure of equilibrium, were when he was tending one of his flocks, alone. He would enter the rhythms of these peaceful creatures, and his mind would slow down, so that he almost felt that he was one of them, with no past or future, lying down in green pastures, standing beside the still waters, walking through the valley of the shadow of death, which to him meant the whole earth, and fearing no evil, since their minds were incapable of projecting a future. Then, with a jolt, he would become human again, as he remembered Joseph, or even Rachel, greeting him with a smile and an embrace when he got home, and the mental act of comparing the past to the present would shatter his peace.

The famine didn't deepen his sorrow—nothing could have done that; it was too deep to deepen. Actually, the famine brought him out of himself, since he had to take measures to ensure his family's survival. Things looked grim. The lakes and streams were drying up. There had been no rain that winter or the one before, and day after day the sun blazed down onto the parched fields. The animals were gaunt; you could see their ribs sticking out. The humans looked gaunt too. Children wept from hunger. People were frightened. At night Jacob would lie awake with anxiety, helplessly trying to find a solution. Sometimes, listening to the wails that came from the women's tents, he would feel overwhelmed with guilt, as if he had broken some solemn promise to God.

One day he learned that there was grain available in Egypt, enough to be sold to foreigners. So he said to his sons, "Go to

Egypt. Hurry. Buy grain for us, so that we don't all starve to death."

Ten of Joseph's brothers went to Egypt to buy grain. (Since the rations to foreigners were being distributed on a per capita basis, this called for the presence of as many of them as possible.) Only Benjamin stayed in Canaan. Jacob was afraid that he would meet with some disaster if he went. Benjamin was thirty-two now, with three wives of his own and ten sons, but at times Jacob still treated him like a child.

In the months immediately after Joseph's disappearance, Jacob had clung to Benjamin as a shipwrecked sailor clings to a spar. He could hardly bear to let him out of his sight. He was distraught every time the boy got sick or returned late from an errand. The thought that he might lose the last remnant on earth of his beloved Rachel tore at his heart and woke him in the middle of the night. Benjamin was forbidden to travel anywhere that would require him to sleep away from home. This fear-encrusted attention was onerous for the young man, and he had periods when he resented his father and was even furious at his mother and Joseph for dying and leaving him on earth as their poor substitute. But almost always when he appeared before Jacob every morning and evening to receive his blessing and a kiss on the forehead, it wasn't a tyrant he saw, but a frightened old man who desperately loved him.

The Brothers Travel to Egypt

IN THE FIRST DAYS OF THE FAMINE, Joseph stationed interpreters at the border with Canaan, men who could speak the local languages (Jebusite, Kenite, Girgashite, and so on). One of them was proficient in Hebrew. He was entrusted with special instructions: as soon as any Hebrew-speaking travelers arrived, he was to send immediate word to Joseph and bring them directly to his palace.

It took seven days for the brothers to reach Egypt with their thirty donkeys. At the border they found a refugee camp: thousands of tents, starving children with glazed eyes, old men slumped over in despair.

Egypt looked as barren as Canaan. Nothing was growing in the arid fields. The sun loomed overhead without the relief of a single cloud.

But at least the Egyptians weren't starving. They looked fairly healthy, and the brothers could see no walking corpses, skeletons wrapped in skin, as among the poor of their own land. People here seemed to be going about their business as in normal times. The guards assigned to take the brothers to Memphis were in good spirits. One of them kept whistling a cheerful tune.

The seat of government and the royal palace had been moved from Memphis to Thebes centuries before, but Memphis, known then as Ankh-Tawy, the Life of the Two Lands, was still Egypt's most important commercial center. It stood at the mouth of the Nile delta, and it was the obvious site for Joseph's palace. On their way to it, the brothers passed the largest building in the city, the ancient temple of Ptah, lord of truth, master of justice, "the god with the beautiful face," the demiurge who had thought the world into existence. They had never seen such magnificence before.

Equanimity

JOSEPH HAD ARRIVED AT A STATE of spiritual maturity in which stressful emotions such as anger, sadness, and disappointment no longer arose—or arose so rarely that he could count the years between episodes. ("Seizures," Asenath would call them.) His default state of calm was extremely steady, and he could depend on it from day to day, from hour to hour. It was an inner equipoise that was unaffected by pleasure or pain, gain or loss, praise or blame. He was detached from events in the sense that they no longer disturbed his mind, but this detachment was not a mode of separation; it was a mode of freedom. It allowed him to deeply connect with people, whether they were in trouble or at peace. No one ever experienced Joseph as aloof.

Equanimity is sometimes thought of as a dry or cold state of being, devoid of feeling. It's not. Joseph's inner life was filled with passionate emotions: deep love for his family, intense aesthetic pleasure, the joy of playing with or against Asenath's nimble wit, wholehearted devotion to Pharaoh

and to Joseph's new country, the thrill of letting his intelligence gallop through an intellectual challenge, fulfillment in
difficult work well done, and always, throughout the day,
gratitude for the generosity of the given world. When an emotion surged through him and his heart beat faster—as when
he was making love with Asenath, or when he sat beside her
during the birth of each son, on the edge of attention, filled
with compassion for her pain—he was always, at the same
time, in touch with the seemingly bottomless reservoir of
calm that lay beneath it all.

During the famine, in spite of all the human misery that
was constantly being reported to him, he never questioned the
goodness of the vast intelligence that was the source of everything, because he had questioned it thoroughly while he was
in the pit, so many years before—had submitted it to a doubt
that was like a consuming fire. His trust had become second
nature, as intimate as breathing.

Though he didn't yet know it, his brothers' arrival was about
to stir powerful emotions in him: rejoicing, love, fulfillment,
compassion, tears of pure resonance with no sorrow in them.
But in the midst of all these emotions, he would always remain the observer, the listener—amused, serene, both in and
out of the game and watching and wondering at it.

They Bow Down Before Joseph

JOSEPH AND ASENATH WERE HAVING their noon meal in the private dining room. It was just the two of them, with Manasseh and Ephraim, aged five and three, who were being particularly well-behaved young gentlemen today. Two nursemaids stood there on call, as well as a footman who served the meal, which was a simple one of smoked goose with berry sauce and sautéed vegetables, a modest salad, and fruit. The fruits and vegetables came from Joseph's personal greenhouse, which, even during the famine, was expertly cared for. For dessert, there was a lemon soufflé. (Note: Chocolate and vanilla wouldn't be available in the Eastern Hemisphere for another three thousand years.)

As they were finishing, the butler entered and bowed to Joseph. "Your Highness," he said, "there is a message from the border. Ten Hebrew-speaking barbarians have arrived, wishing to buy grain. They will be here today."

Joseph stood up. He exchanged a look with Asenath, then quickly followed the butler out of the room.

"Tell the Hebrew interpreter to meet me in the Great Hall, an hour from now," he said.

The butler bowed and hurried off, a little confused. Wasn't Hebrew the viceroy's native tongue?

On his way to the Great Hall, Joseph's heart was beating even faster than when he had received the news, and he felt a warmth rising to his cheeks. Could these be his brothers, finally? But why ten and not eleven? Was Benjamin not with them? Was he dead? Was another of them dead? But it had to be them. This had to be the beginning of the endgame. "Dear God," he prayed, "if it be Your will . . ." He could get no further. He didn't need to.

Two and a half hours later, when the brothers were ushered into the Great Hall, they bowed to the ground before him. Joseph recognized Reuben immediately: the same large, rugged body, the same face, though of course much older now, with hair and beard turned gray. Then he recognized them all.

"Where have you come from?" he said in Egyptian. His tone was harsh. The interpreter imitated the harshness in Hebrew.

"From Canaan, my lord," Judah said as they lay stretched out on the marble floor, not daring to look up. "We have come to buy grain."

Joseph remembered his dreams. He had remembered them many times before, but now, with his brothers prostrate before him, the memory was so vivid that he felt as if reality had superimposed itself onto the dreams, or vice versa, so that it was the sheaves, or the stars, that were bowing down before him now in the form of his brothers. He was deeply moved.

The feeling was one of fulfillment, not of triumph or

vindication. None of this was personal. Here he was, sitting on the viceregal throne, amid the barely imaginable splendor of his court, surrounded by hundreds of dignitaries, ministers, bureaucrats, fan bearers, and heralds, all standing at attention to carry out his commands, and he hadn't arrived here through any intention or effort of his own. He was just an actor. The whole drama of sin and redemption, of death and rebirth, was being played out *through* him, and all his suffering and success had been present in embryo in those dreams. Time had collapsed. The arrogant, innocent seventeen-year-old boy had, in a flash, reappeared in this thirty-eight-year-old man's body; the coat of many colors had become the white linen robe of office; the vigorous young shepherds had turned into gaunt middle-aged men with weather-beaten skin, grizzled beards, and eyes dimmed by suffering and deprivation.

What next? He had to get his brothers to bring Benjamin and their father to join him here. How he could do that he didn't know. He had many unanswered questions. Were his brothers sorry for what they had done? Was he meant to play a role in their repentance?

One thing was clear: it was not yet time to reveal himself.

More Harsh Words

AS SOON AS JOSEPH GAVE THEM PERMISSION, the brothers picked themselves up from the floor. They were twenty feet away from the dais, flanked by officers of the guard. Joseph scanned their faces, his chin cupped in his right hand.

They looked weary. He wanted to finish the drama soon, but there was still too much uncertainty. Was Jacob alive? Was Benjamin? Had they been persecuting the boy? Did they even remember their crime?

He couldn't simply sell them their portion of grain and let them go. He needed to wait until he had a clearer sense of things. There was no real harm in speaking harshly. It would cause them some emotional pain, but just in passing, and it would earn him time. He knew very well how to act with gruff authority, since he had perfected that role in his dealings with the recalcitrant rich.

He would have to be careful now. As he looked into the frightened faces, he would have to keep close watch on the subtler layers of his thinking, so that he wouldn't burst into tears at his brothers' distress or into exultant laughter that they had finally, finally come. All right. He was not Joseph now; he was Zaphnath-paneakh, Viceroy of All Egypt, Bearer of the Royal Seals, Pharaoh's Father and Sole Companion, Overseer of the Granaries, First Royal Herald, and Right Hand of the Lord of the Two Lands. He scowled. He leaned forward in his chair. He pointed his finger.

"You are spies!" he shouted. "You have come to search out the weak points in the imperial defenses!"

"No, n-no, my lord," Levi stammered. (The interpreter stammered as well.) "W-we are not spies. We are simple shepherds. We have come to buy food. We are honest men, my lord. We aren't spies."

"You lie! You have come to search out our weaknesses!"

"My lord, my lord," Judah said, "we are twelve brothers, sons of one man back in Canaan. But the youngest of us is at home with our father, and one of us is gone."

"Silence!" Joseph shouted. "*I* say you are spies, and this is how you will be tested. You will not leave this place unless your youngest brother comes here, to prove that you are telling the truth. Choose one of you to go and bring your brother back to me. The rest will remain in prison until your story is proven true.* Otherwise, I swear by Pharaoh, you will all be executed as spies."

Guards surrounded them and quick-marched them to the Hall of Detention.

---

* Rabbi Yossi ben Torta of Hazor said, "It was only fair for them to be imprisoned. As it is said, 'He who is burdened with blood-guilt shall flee to the pit.'" (Prov. 28:17) Rabbi Yochanan the Elder of Sampho said, "Joseph wanted them to meditate on their sin. As it is said, 'For the Lord hears the needy, / and does not despise his prisoners.'" (Ps. 69:33)

"Let It Be Simeon"

JOSEPH MADE SURE THAT THEY WERE physically comfortable in prison, but he had each of them placed in a separate cell— not as a punishment, but as an opportunity for reflection. If each brother were to face the imminent prospect of death, he might be forced to reckon with his conscience. Joseph was not trying to punish them. He took no pleasure in their fear. He was just doing his best to understand what God had presented him with.

Over the next three days, as he discussed it with Asenath, the situation became clearer in his mind. He realized that he had been hasty in saying he would detain nine of them. There was no compelling reason for it, and the news would be that much more difficult for his father to bear. Besides, the families would be desperate for food, and he wanted to send back as much as he could, as quickly as he could. He needed to detain one man only. Let it be Simeon or Levi, the biggest troublemakers. Let it be Simeon.

In the Cells

"I HAVE DISCOVERED," THE PHILOSOPHER Pascal wrote, "that all human misery comes from one fact: that we are unable to sit at ease alone in a room." This insight is more radical than you might at first imagine.

The solitary confinement was excruciating for the brothers. Pacing back and forth in the narrow cells, which were equipped only with cot, water pitcher, and bowl for human waste, all of them went wild with fear, not only for their own lives but for the lives of their starving families. How had their mission been so wretchedly diverted? What in the world had they done to turn the great lord against them? Were they all going to die now? *We have failed our father,* Reuben thought. It was the shame of this failure that burned inside him most painfully. There was an ironic sense of justice in this, he realized. *I didn't care about Father when we sold Joseph. Now I do, and this caring is my greatest sorrow.*

The lord's presence was august and strange, yet there was something familiar about him amid all his splendor. Each man felt disoriented. Everything had lost its name; nothing was recognizable. Old memories floated up to the surface of consciousness, old guilts, *the* old guilt, the vision of Joseph battered and thrown into the pit, the voice of Joseph pleading with them, the voice of their father as he sobbed inconsolably for his lost darling. They felt that they were wandering in a labyrinth of confusion. Each man tried to find a way out. Each man failed.

Tears of Joy

ON THE THIRD DAY, JOSEPH SUMMONED the brothers from the Hall of Detention. Four spear-bearing guards marched them into the Great Hall, where Joseph sat on his throne. He gestured to the guards, who pushed the brothers toward him, then stepped back two paces. Reuben and Judah were the only ones who seemed to be in any control of their emotions. The rest looked terrified. Some of the younger men were trembling.

Joseph leaned forward. He scanned their faces, slowly. Then he said, "Do what I command, and your lives will be spared. I am a fair man. I just need to test whether you have been honest with me. One of you will stay here in prison as a hostage, while the rest take grain to your families. But you must bring me your youngest brother, to prove that you are telling the truth. Do this, and I will let you all live."

The brothers turned to one another with relief and alarm. Judah said, "This must be a punishment for what we did to our brother Joseph. We threw him into a pit, and we saw his anguish when he pleaded with us, but we wouldn't listen. That is why this anguish has overtaken us." The brothers all murmured their assent. (They didn't realize that Joseph understood their words.)

As he felt tears rise in his throat, Joseph got up and hurried off the dais and through the door to his office. He hadn't wept for twenty-two years, almost as long as he hadn't heard the sound of the Hebrew language. Now, as he reached his desk, the tears began to pour down his cheeks. He didn't try to stop them. His heart was bursting with gratitude. So they *did* remember. They *did* repent.

For five minutes he sat at his desk, sobbing, with his head resting on his folded arms. Then he stood up, went over to the basin, washed and dried his face, and walked toward the door. He knew what to do now.

An Unwelcome Surprise

WHEN JOSEPH WAS ABLE TO FACE THEM again, he pointed to Simeon. A guard hurried over and shackled his arms and legs with iron chains. The chains echoed the decision with dull clinks.

Then Joseph gave his steward orders to fill their sacks with grain, give them provisions for their trip, put back each one's purchase money into his pack, and send them away.

He had thought of this little surprise at the last moment, in a kind of inspiration. It had immediately seemed like the right thing to do, though it wasn't until after the brothers had left that he understood why he had done it. He was sending a message to his father. He couldn't reveal himself now, nor could he find a way to urge Jacob to send Benjamin; the old man would show ferocious resistance to that. But he *could* arrange for something uncanny, something that might say to his father, "Stop. Consider." Uncanniness was sometimes a signature of God's action, and Joseph not only possessed the signature seal of Pharaoh, he could also sign this event in God's name. Whether Jacob would recognize his message Joseph had no way of knowing. Perhaps fear for Benjamin would dull his father's ears and put blinders over his eyes. But Joseph had to make the attempt.

He commanded his steward to place nine of the money bags at the bottom of the packs and one at the top. This would serve the dual purpose of signing the event for his brothers and, when they arrived, signing it, in even bolder strokes, for his father as well.*

The brothers loaded the grain onto their donkeys and left. After a long day of travel, they stopped to rest outside a village halfway to the Great Green Water, had their meal, and, eager to get home as quickly as possible, decided to sleep for just a few hours. As they were bedding down, Issachar opened his pack to get fodder for his donkey, and there, at the top of the pack, impossibly, was his bag of silver.

"Oh my God!" he shouted. "The money! It's here, in my pack!"

They stared at one another. *What has God done to us?* each man thought.

---

* Rabbi Shela bar Menahem of Sepphoris said, "He did this to stir up in each brother the sense that God had appointed it. As it is said, 'He took a bag of money with him and will come home on the day appointed.'" (Prov. 7:20) Rabbi Tarfon the Ironmonger said, "It was to show them that mercy can't be bought. As it is said, 'You shall be redeemed without money.'" (Isa. 52:3)

Jacob's Response

AND SO THE BROTHERS RETURNED HOME, their thirty donkeys loaded with sacks of grain. As soon as they entered their father's tent, they told him what had happened and what was required of him. The donkeys waited outside, steaming and pungent.

Jacob barely listened to them. What they were saying made no sense. He didn't *want* to find sense in it. He could see only the loss. At least his family wouldn't starve for now. But how could they ask him to let Benjamin go? Did they want to tear his flesh with their teeth, like a pack of wild dogs? Let Simeon rot in Egypt. Let them all go to Egypt, or go to hell. Benjamin would stay right here.

"Take Him, If You Must"

BUT THE FAMINE REMAINED SEVERE. There was no rain. The sun blazed down every day, its brutal force unassuaged by the mercy of clouds. The animals grew weak. Some died. Four of the slaves died as well, and others were too ill to carry out their duties.

After three months, when most of the grain from Egypt was gone, Jacob called all ten sons to his tent. It was a hot morning in October, during what should have been the autumn harvest. Leah came to the tent as well, along with Bilhah and Zilpah. They all looked frightened.

Jacob waited in silence as they sat down or knelt before him. When everyone was settled, he stood up to speak. "It can't go on this way," he said gravely. "The famine is only getting worse. The children are wasting away. You have to go back to Egypt, the nine of you, and buy us more grain, and bring Simeon home."

Judah stood up and bowed to him. "Father," he said, "we all hear you and agree. But the great lord warned us not to return by ourselves—don't you remember? He said we would be put to death unless we brought Benjamin with us next time. So how can we go without him? Please, Father, send Benjamin in my care. I promise I will bring him back to you. And Father, we should start right away, so that we all don't starve to death."

Judah's experience with Tamar had awakened him to his own frailties. He had come so close to executing an innocent woman that he could never again have total confidence in the thought *I am right*. Rightness, and righteousness too, were positions far more precarious than he had realized, and they needed to be tested in every way before he could again act in good conscience. Life itself was more precarious than he had realized. He felt that he had somehow forfeited his own the moment he had decided to burn Tamar. So volunteering as a surety for his little brother wasn't difficult for him. He was willing to sacrifice everything for his sake.

Benjamin didn't say a word. It wasn't his place to speak. When he was very young, he had lived in the shadow of Joseph's brilliance. After Joseph disappeared, he had to endure the burden of his father's deflected love, which was actually a mode of despair. He had played the role of Jacob's lifeline for so many years now—ever since he was eleven—that it felt like a part of his identity. And while he occasionally found it galling, he understood why his father treated him like a boy, even though he was the father of ten sons himself. The old man needed someone to cling to, and he, after all, was a son of Rachel, the beloved, though mutedly, compared with his brother Joseph. Jacob would sometimes call him to his tent and gaze at him with such longing that it brought tears to Benjamin's eyes. How could he not feel a boundless compassion for the old man, a compassion that made the indignity of his own situation seem almost trivial?

Jacob pondered for a day and a night, so sick with anxiety that he couldn't eat or sleep. All the grandchildren were warned to keep away from his tent, and if they had to come near, for God's sake to be quiet. Leah came to see him in the afternoon, bringing bread, lamb stew, and wine, but when she tried to feed him, he pushed her hand away. She stayed with him for two hours as he sat with his head between his palms, staring down into the dirt.

The next morning, he summoned the brothers and the women again. With a sob in his voice, he turned to Judah and said, "Take him, if you must." Tears streamed down his face. He had to wait a few minutes before he could speak again. "Take him with you. Go back to Egypt. And may God Almighty move the great lord to deal compassionately with you and let Benjamin come home to me again."

Gifts

THERE WAS NO OTHER OPTION. For a day and a night Jacob had wrestled with the necessity for sending Benjamin. This time God had defeated him.

Still, they would have to take every precaution. They would bear gifts, and the gifts would be extravagant, since that was the protocol when appearing before a great lord. Jacob's wealth was mostly in livestock; it would have been difficult to drive sheep or goats to Egypt, even if the animals had been healthy, but he still had stores, sadly dwindled now, of the local products that were most in demand throughout the region. The land of Canaan was famous for its almonds, pistachios, spices, and myrrh; and its honey—a thick syrup made not by bees but from dates and grapes—sweetened the lives of the well-to-do from Egypt to Mesopotamia.

But the silver: they would have to neutralize the reappearance of their silver shekels. At the very least they would have to return the money, with excuses and abject apologies. The great lord didn't know God's uncanny ways, and he might think . . . But who knew what he might think? Their position had to be one of humility, humiliation even. Jacob knew about self-abasement. He had groveled like a beggar before his brother, Esau, who in the twenty years since Jacob's flight from home had become a rich and powerful chieftain and who Jacob had feared still harbored a murderous resentment toward him for his theft of the Blessing. Jacob had eaten the dust at Esau's feet. He had squeaked out his gratitude at having his miserable life spared. That was the mercy he had prayed for back then. Now again, perhaps, in the guise of this powerful ruler, God might let them all live.

With the Steward

SO THE TEN BROTHERS TOOK THE GIFTS, and double the amount of money, and they set out. All of them were extremely anxious, but Benjamin's anxiety was tempered with a sense of exhilaration at being away from home and seeing new lands for the first time in his life.

When they arrived at the Egyptian border, they were again assigned to the Hebrew-speaking interpreter, who recognized the barbarians from their first visit. Reuben explained that they had exhausted their supply of grain and had come to buy more. "We'll be regular customers," Levi added, with a forced smile.

Four guards escorted them to Joseph's palace. It took half a day for them to arrive. Then they were handed over to Joseph's steward. "We beg your pardon, sir," Judah said to him, "but we came down here to buy grain once before, a few months ago. When we returned home, each of us found his money in his pack. So we have brought it back. We also brought more money to buy grain. We don't know how the money got into our packs."

The steward said, "Don't worry. Everything is as it should be. I did receive your money when you were here before. It must have been your god, the god of your father, who hid the money in your packs."

The steward was in on the plan; in fact, he was the one who had put the money into their packs. Many times he had heard Joseph mention his nameless god, and he was not above improvising here, speaking as his master might have spoken. Besides, it was the truth, as he understood it. His master's god acted through humans in the same way as the Aten shines down upon all beings; the principle was the same, whether it was from the outside or the inside. These unshorn Asiatics, who looked so wild and barbarous—though when he examined them more closely he could see the resemblance to his master, especially in the youngest one—didn't understand yet. They believed that they were in danger. When he told them that he had the money, he could see the relief on their faces.

It was time now for the interlude. His master had a genius for detail. Everything was ready: towels and water basins, fodder for the animals, a splendid banquet in the Dining Hall. Banquets were extremely rare during the famine, even for Pharaoh, and were reserved only for the most essential state occasions. This one would be beyond the most extravagant dreams of these barbarians. Perhaps that was his master's point.

He could hardly wait to see what would happen next.

Benjamin

THE STEWARD LED THE BROTHERS to the Great Hall and told them that they would be dining with His Highness the Viceroy at noon.

Benjamin looked around. He could hardly believe his eyes. The hall was lined with huge multicolored columns, and the walls and ceiling too were ablaze with color: images of birds, beasts, ancient pharaohs and their consorts, geometric patterns in blue, green, red, and yellow, gods with the heads of hawks or lions or crocodiles. At one end of the hall, a golden throne was flanked by two golden jackals lying at attention with their paws stretched in front of them and their large pointed ears unfurled like sails in the wind. Dozens of spear-bearing guards stood along the walls, naked to the waist, with thick bronze bands around their upper arms.

Then Simeon was brought in. Levi ran up and threw his arms around him. The other nine crowded close. Simeon told them that his chains had been taken off minutes after he had been led away three months before. He had been moved to a comfortable room in the palace. And though he had been under constant scrutiny, confined to his room and a small courtyard, he had been treated well, fed well, and allowed recreation and exercise. They had also offered him books, but of course he couldn't read. The solitude had been painful, though. He had missed his family, more than he could say.

After half an hour, Joseph arrived. They presented him with their gifts and bowed to the ground before him.

"How is your father?" Joseph said. "Is he still alive? Is he well?"

"Yes, he is both, my lord," Judah answered.

Joseph looked at Benjamin, his own mother's son, and said, "This must be your youngest brother." And to Benjamin: "May God be gracious to you, my son."

The man had to be Benjamin. Still, Joseph was shocked. He stared at him, trying to make the thirty-two-year-old face fit the memory of his brother as a rosy eleven-year-old, a boy who adored him and followed him everywhere. Anxiety and deprivation had faded the boy's flesh and dimmed his eyes, but as Joseph kept looking, the two mental images—past and present—approached each other and merged. He could feel deep emotion rising in him again, love and compassion and gratitude for being here at the end of this journey, an end that was contiguous with its beginning, like the ritual serpent biting its tail.

It was too much to contain. He hurried out of the room. He had to exert all his willpower to keep the tears from spilling out before he reached the door to his office.

◇

The Banquet

AFTER HE HAD WEPT TO HIS HEART's content, Joseph washed his face, composed himself, and came out. He had the butler lead everyone to the Dining Hall, which was almost as large a room and just as splendid. There they were joined by several dozen Egyptian dignitaries, who had been hastily invited for the sake of appearances. Two long tables were laid out with elaborate settings of crystal, silver, and linen.

Once the Egyptians had been seated, he ordered the butler to seat his brothers in order of their ages, the eldest first and the youngest last. As he did, Simeon gave Levi a silent poke. Gad and Asher exchanged glances of bewilderment. Reuben leaned over to Judah and whispered that the great lord must have some kind of supernatural insight. It was one thing for him to see that he, Reuben, was the eldest, or that Levi was older than Zebulun. But how could he tell that Simeon was older than Levi (they looked like twins), or that Judah was older than Dan, who had been born just four months after him, or that Naphtali was older than Gad, Asher than Issachar? Yet he hadn't hesitated and hadn't made a single mistake. Something uncanny was happening again.

The footmen served Joseph first, on the dais, where because of his exalted position he ate alone. Then they served the brothers and the Egyptian guests, separately, since Egyptians weren't permitted to eat with Hebrews. (Hebrews were considered unclean, and eating with them would have been what the priests called an abomination. For Egyptians, other nations were not quite human. There were exceptions, such as Joseph, but these were rare. Barbarians ate cow flesh, and cows were sacred. Sheep, too, mustn't be eaten under any circumstances. This made Hebrews repulsive to any decent, right-thinking person.)

So the brothers feasted and drank with Joseph. There were pitchers of ale, lager, and stout on every table, and sommeliers circulated, pouring wines from the finest old vintages. After the hors d'oeuvre—roast pork in pomegranate sauce (the concept "kosher" wouldn't exist for another four hundred years)— there was a seafood course of raw oysters, grilled lobster, and six kinds of fish in a mustard/white wine sauce, then main courses of roast goose, partridge, and venison, with grains and vegetables, followed by a fruit course, ices, two dozen kinds of pastry, and dessert wines, brandy, and liqueurs.

The lavishness of it all was beyond their grasp. Only Judah and Benjamin showed any moderation. Most of the brothers gorged themselves and got drunk, joking, laughing, tossing bread pellets at one another from across the table, and paying no attention to the musicians or the dancing girls, or to the splendidly clothed Egyptian noblemen who from the other table glared at them with undisguised contempt.

◇

The Silver Cup

AFTER THE BANQUET WAS OVER and the brothers were comfortably settled in the guest bedrooms, Joseph said to his steward, "Fill the men's packs with grain, and put my silver cup in the pack of the youngest one."

The point was to choose a valuable object, and there was nothing more valuable to the Egyptians than a divination cup. Joseph didn't believe in divination, but everyone else in Egypt did. As with the other psychic disciplines, there were hundreds of textbooks, academies, and self-confident experts, and three major schools of thought: oilism, wineism, and waterism, among which the arguments about the efficacy of their respective methods dated back thousands of years, to the earliest dynasties. (Joseph had seen experts from all three schools declaim before Pharaoh and fail in equally undetectable ways, with prophecies that used vagueness as a methodology.) On rare occasions, when he thought that a decision of his would cause more than the usual resistance, Joseph used this superstition to his political advantage. He had bought an ancient, historic divination cup, a masterpiece of the silversmith's art, which had belonged to one of the priestly dynasties for centuries, and on these occasions he would fill it with the prescribed portion of wine, drop the prescribed portion of oil into it, gaze solemnly at the patterns, and solemnly announce his conclusions to the exasperated rich.

But, you may be wondering, why all this drama around the cup? Why didn't Joseph reveal himself to his brothers in the Great Hall or during the banquet? Did he really need to test them in this way, pushing them to the brink of despair?

Well, if you play it out, you'll see how much more satisfying a conclusion our story has with this test than without it. Joseph was an artist of events, and his intuition here was as aesthetic as it was moral. He didn't want half-knowledge and lukewarm acceptance. If his brothers were still callous, he wanted to know that. They had changed; they had repented; but how deep did their contrition go? How would they react if Benjamin seemed to be in mortal danger? Would they come to his defense? Or would they be willing to break their father's heart all over again? The test was not only for his sake, it was for theirs as well. It would give them the opportunity to reveal themselves to themselves as well as to him. His own self-revelation would have an entirely different quality if it was made to men who were sincerely sorry for what they had done, rather than to men with hearts still calcified in envy and resentment.

Found!

DAYLIGHT CAME, AND AFTER THE MEN were sent off with their donkeys, Joseph said to his steward, "Follow them. When you catch up, say, 'Shame on you! Why have you stolen my master's silver cup, the one he looks into to see what lies hidden?'" Joseph was clear about cause and effect, and in that sense he could indeed see what lay hidden. It had nothing to do with the silver cup, of course. But he spoke in the language of psychic powers in order to ratchet up the pressure on his brothers. This was the drama's climax. With all his heart he wanted them to pass the test.

The steward took along a dozen guards. When he caught up with the brothers, he repeated Joseph's words. Reuben said, "How can you accuse us of such a thing, sir?"

"It's outrageous!" Levi shouted. "How dare you!" He took a step toward the man, but Simeon caught his arm and held him back.

Judah said, "Sir, haven't we proved our honesty by bringing back the money we found in our packs, all the way from

Canaan? How could we repay your master with such wickedness?"

There was a collective murmur of agreement.

"If you find the cup with any of us," Reuben said, "go ahead and put that man to death, and make the rest of us slaves."

The steward nodded gravely. "What you propose is fair," he said. "Still, if I find the cup with any of you, only that man will be made a slave. The rest of you will go free."

Each of them quickly took down his pack and opened it. The steward searched all the packs. He found the cup in Benjamin's.

How? Who? Why?

NONE OF THE BROTHERS KNEW; only Benjamin did. Their minds shuttled between doubt and conviction. Could he have done it? No. Yes. *How* could he have done it and gotten them into such trouble? Well, if it was his fault, maybe they should just leave him here. But that would kill their father. But it was not as if they still had a choice. Or was it God who had put the silver cup in his pack, as with the money? However this had happened, it spelled disaster. Reuben wanted to bite his tongue. Judah was even more appalled than the others. He had made a solemn promise to his father, and now there would be no way to keep it.

For Benjamin, however, there was no question of a theft. He pondered. Denying the theft would do no good, since the evidence would so clearly make him a liar. He knew to keep silent when there was nothing useful to say.

It might be God who had acted here, or it might be a human. If a human, it couldn't have been one of his brothers. Who, then? The Egyptians were all under the command of the great lord, who had seemed to show such partiality to him. So in the end it would come down to the great lord.

But why would he have played such a nasty trick on them all? To make him his slave? Benjamin couldn't believe that. The great lord seemed like a decent, generous man. He had to know that detaining Benjamin would kill their father. He would never do something like that.

Then why had he done it?

Judah Reflects

THE GREAT HALL OF JOSEPH'S PALACE was filled with dignitaries and government officials. Clerks fluttered about with unsigned documents. The Fan Bearer on the Viceroy's Right and the Fan Bearer on the Viceroy's Left stood holding their tall black-and-white ostrich-feather fans upright on either side of Joseph's throne. The fan bearers' function was purely ceremonial, even on warm days like this. It would have been beneath their dignity to actually wave the fans.

The brothers, frightened and dejected, were escorted into the hall by a phalanx of guards. When they came within twenty-five feet of the dais where Joseph's throne stood, they stopped and prostrated themselves before him, palms and foreheads pressed against the cold marble slabs of the floor. The dignitaries and government officials looked at them with disgust. There was whispering and hushed laughter.

"How could you do this?" Joseph said. The interpreter echoed his tone of grave displeasure. "Don't you know that a man like me sees what lies hidden?"

"What can we tell you, my lord?" Judah said, lifting his head to speak. "How can we claim that we are innocent? God has uncovered our crime."

Judah saw no point in denying the theft. How the cup had found its way into Benjamin's pack—whether it was by supernatural intervention or whether Benjamin had suddenly lost his wits—was irrelevant, though how Benjamin could even have gotten near the cup, with all those soldiers standing at attention around the dining table, was more than Judah could comprehend. He believed they were all innocent of this crime, but that didn't make them innocent. For more than two decades he had been waiting for the other crime to be punished. God is subtle in His ways, but He is not careless, and He brings all things to their balance in His own sweet time. Sooner or later there is always a balancing, as Judah had learned abruptly in the almost fatal mistake he had made with Tamar, which had shaken him to the core.

Now, devastating as it was to contemplate the possible consequences of this theft, he felt a strange relief about it. God was certainly at work here. He was showing them all what they had been too immature, too craven, to realize when they had succumbed to their jealousy and rage. How could they have been so brutal as to shut their father's grief out of their minds when they attacked his favorite son? Well, once again God was holding their father's grief before them, this time about Benjamin. It was horrible to behold. They would have to relive it when they went home, only this time it would be even worse. And the fault would be Judah's alone.

"I Am Joseph"

"MAY WE HAVE YOUR LORDSHIP'S PERMISSION to stand?" said Judah.

"Yes, yes," Joseph said with an elegant wave of his right hand. The interpreter waved his right hand as well.

"We come here as your slaves, my lord," Judah continued after they were all on their feet, "not only our brother who was found with the cup, but the rest of us as well."

"No," Joseph said, "that wouldn't be right. Only the man who was found with the cup will be taken as my slave. The rest of you may go back to your father in peace."

But there was no peace in the offer. It wasn't possible for them to leave: the news of Benjamin's enslavement would kill the old man. Nor was it possible to stay in Egypt, since if they did, their families would starve.

Then Judah stepped forward and said, "I beg your indulgence, my lord. Let your humble servant speak a few words, please, and listen to what he says, even though you are as great as Pharaoh."

"Speak," Joseph said, leaning forward.

"You asked us about our family, my lord. We told you that we had an agèd father and a child of his old age, a young man whose full brother is dead, so that he alone is left of his mother's children. And you said to us, 'Bring him to me. Unless he comes with you, you will not be admitted.' When we told your words to our father, he said, 'My wife bore me two sons. One was taken from me, and now you want to take this one too, and if he met with some disaster, you would send my white head down to the grave in anguish.'"

Judah paused for a few moments. Joseph was doing everything he could to hold back the tears that were rising in his throat and behind his eyes.

"And so, my lord," Judah continued, "if I go back to our father and he sees that his son isn't with us, he will die of grief, and it will be my fault. I told him that I would take care of his son. I promised I would bring him home. And so I beg you, my lord, please, let me stay here as your slave instead of this man, and let him leave with the rest of us. If my brother is not with me, how can I go back to my father? How can I bear to see the anguish that will consume him?"*

Joseph could no longer control himself. "Leave my presence!" he shouted. "Everyone!"

The viceregal fan bearers and the dozen chief ministers filed out first; next, the fifty deputies and heads of departments, carrying their ostrich-skin briefcases full of papyrus work. Last went the three hundred scribes, heralds, and pages, who

---

* Rabbi Shmuel the Weaver of Gennesaret said, "Because he loved his father more than he loved himself, Judah became the Suffering Servant. As it is said, 'He was willing to bear the sins of many.'" (Isa. 53:12)

crowded toward the front door with a clatter of sandals. A few, unable to master their curiosity, glanced over their shoulders on the way out, at Joseph standing to the right of his throne and weeping in silence, but immediately they had to turn their heads forward as they were swept along toward the front door.

So no one else was there when he made himself known to his brothers. But many of the Egyptians stood listening outside the door.

"אֲנִי יוֹסֵף—*Ani Yosef*," he said. ("I am Joseph.") These were the first Hebrew words he had spoken in almost twenty-two years. He hadn't heard his own name once in all that time, and it stirred nameless emotions in him, sounds and smells, his mother's voice singing to him as she held him in her arms, the feel of his father's palms on his forehead as he blessed him— memories suddenly so vivid that they reached down and drew up tears from the depths of him.

At first he could barely see his brothers through the mist that filled his eyes. Then he was able to observe them. Shock, incomprehension, terror. He would have to say more.

Stupefied

"IS MY FATHER REALLY ALIVE?" Joseph said. (He spoke Hebrew with a slight Egyptian accent.)

The brothers couldn't answer. What had just happened was impossible. How could the great lord say he was their brother? Was he testing them? Was he joking? Was he out of his mind? And how had he learned their humble language? Their minds whirled with unanswerable questions. They were stupefied. All they could do was stare.

"Come closer to me," Joseph said. And when they came closer: "I am your brother Joseph, whom you sold into Egypt."

VI.

The Way of Forgiveness

No Blame

FIRST HE HAD TO PROVE TO THEM who he was. So: their crime first. Who else but he could know that? He wished not to exaggerate or diminish it, but to state it plainly, without judgment, and move on.

The next thing was to let these terrified men know that he had forgiven them, that he felt no anger or resentment, no residue from the event, and that he was standing before them with an open heart. Actually, *forgiveness* was an inaccurate word for what he was experiencing, since it implies that a magnanimous "I" grants something to a not-necessarily-deserving "you." It wasn't like that at all. He wasn't granting anything or even doing anything. He realized that his brothers were guilty, but he also saw the innocence in that guilt. True forgiveness, he had learned, is the realization that there is nothing to forgive. His brothers simply hadn't known what they were doing. And given the violence of their emotions, there was nothing else they could have done.

"Don't be troubled now," Joseph continued, "and don't

blame yourselves for selling me." He paused. This dimension of forgiveness was something he couldn't convey to his brothers, or to anyone else. They would have to discover their own innocence for themselves. The most he could do now was to hint at it, to suggest that they follow his example. If he, who was the apparent victim, didn't blame them, why should they blame themselves? He knew that this reassurance would do little if any good. His brothers would *have* to blame themselves; they wouldn't be able to see their own innocence until their minds slowed down enough to understand their crime in the greater scheme of things. In the meantime, they would necessarily be grieved and angry at themselves, and they would suffer needlessly from a remembered—that is, from an imagined—past that they could neither retract nor change.

There was one last thing to help them understand. "God sent me ahead of you to save lives," he said. Since they all believed in God's power to do whatever He wants—at least, Joseph presumed that they did, being sons of his father—they might be able to realize that there are no accidents in the world. Everything happens according to God's will; everything that happens, whether apparently good or apparently bad, is meant to happen, precisely because it did happen; though the future has infinite possibilities, the past has only one. Therefore, it was God's will that he be sold into Egypt. They couldn't disagree, since this was the obvious truth of it. And how could they blame themselves for something they'd had no control over? Ultimately, it wasn't they who had thrown him into the pit: it was God. It wasn't they who had sold him into Egypt: it was God. God was the only creator in this whole drama; they were simply His instruments, His actors. Their crime had been for the good of them all, though that hadn't been their intention. So there was nothing to reproach themselves for. What they had done as revenge was actually a blessing in the long run. In reality, nothing is as it seems to be through the filter of a fearful mind. Everything, even the most painful experience, turns out to be pure grace.

"For almost two years now the famine has gripped the land," Joseph said, "and there will be five more years without a harvest. But God sent me ahead of you, and He made me a father to Pharaoh, master of his household and ruler over all Egypt. It's important that you understand this. It wasn't you but God who sent me here."

The brothers stared, as if in a trance.

"Hurry back to our father," Joseph continued, "and give him this message: 'God has made me ruler over all Egypt. Come to me right away; you will live in the region of Goshen, and you will be near me, along with your children and grandchildren, your flocks and herds, and all your possessions. I will take care of you there, and I will make sure that you and your family have everything you need during the five years of famine that lie ahead.'"

They seemed to be coming out of their trance now; at least, some of them were nodding in agreement. Judah said, "We will tell him that, my lord."

"You can see for yourselves now," Joseph said, "and my brother Benjamin can see, that I really am Joseph. Tell Father about all the splendor that surrounds me, and tell him about everything you have seen, and bring him to me as quickly as you can."

"Yes, my lord," Judah said.

The food, Joseph thought—that was the most urgent matter. The families must be fed and brought to Goshen. Jacob would be shocked at the news, and incredulous, but he would come around when he was able to hear his sons' account of the wonder of their meeting. He would see the magnificent gifts. And Goshen, after all, was not quite Egypt; it wasn't Egypt in all its unalloyed, intimidating grandeur, and thus it would be easier for Jacob to accept. So when the famine was over, he would be living in a landscape similar to Canaan's: lush meadows with plenty of water. The palace was just a day's journey away, near enough so that they could see each other as often as they wished.

Then Joseph threw his arms around his brother Benjamin and wept, and Benjamin wept too.

A New Beginning

JOSEPH'S HEART WAS OVERFLOWING with love. It wasn't only for Benjamin; it was for them all, all eleven of them.

This was how he had felt toward his brothers as a very young child, before the capacity to impose fixed judgments on the world had established itself in his mind. Now all their history had been wiped clean, and he felt renewed, purified, washed whiter than snow, as if his whole life with them had begun again from the beginning. These dear men, all of them, with their worn, confused, barely comprehending faces and the smell of fear on their skin: how beautiful they were, each one of them! He had to laugh—it was too ridiculous—at the way he in his youthful arrogance had seen them as coarse and stupid, a judgment that simply mirrored back his own coarseness and stupidity at the time, though it was easy to forgive himself, since he had been as innocent as they were, as ignorant of mental cause-and-effect. He had seen only their exteriors; he had never wanted, or been able, to understand who they were beneath the surface of his own perceptions.

He went from one to the other, looking into their eyes, clasping each one in his arms: Dear Judah. Dan. Naphtali, who had once been swift as a deer. Gad. Issachar. Those roughnecks Simeon and Levi. Asher. Zeb.

Reuben was the last brother he embraced, the eldest and tallest of them. His torso was as thick as a tree trunk. His eyes looked out from the depths of sadness. To Joseph, he too seemed beautiful.

Pharaoh Gives His Consent

WHEN THE NEWS ABOUT JOSEPH'S BROTHERS reached Pharaoh, he was pleased. Usually he would flick away any thought of filthy barbarian shepherds crossing the border into the Black Land. But Zaphnath-paneakh had been a savior to him and to all his people, and there was nothing Pharaoh wouldn't do to please him. He had heaped him with wealth and honors, given him a brilliant jewel of a wife, and followed his advice as if Zaphnath-paneakh were a god descended from the heaven of heavens.

So when he heard the news that the brothers had come and that Zaphnath-paneakh had invited them and their father and their families to live in Goshen, Pharaoh immediately gave his consent. He was happy to see his viceroy reunited with the people he loved, barbarians though they were, and if Zaphnath-paneakh's nose was able to endure their stink, more power to him. The rumor was that he had even wept in his brothers' arms—an astonishing image that Pharaoh could hardly believe, since Zaphnath-paneakh was legendary for his sangfroid, even in circumstances of high tension. People said that he had spoken to the barbarians in their own tongue, a series of barks and snorts that, if one forced oneself to imagine a human voice speaking, sounded like a consumptive clearing his throat. Undoubtedly this was an act of mercy on Zaphnath-paneakh's part, since he could easily have spared himself by calling on an interpreter. He was known for his exquisite manners, which put everyone at ease no matter what their social position might be, and he would shift his tone only in his dealings with the rich and powerful, though even with them his harshness took the form of elegant phrases that were as lethal as daggers.

Well, let the family come. Let them be happy together. How many of them could there be?

Back to Canaan

PHARAOH SENT JOSEPH A MESSAGE. The thin papyrus scroll was tied with a red ribbon and sealed in purple wax with the imperial scarab.

> To our esteemed viceroy, Zaphnath-paneakh, Bearer of the Royal Seals, Pharaoh's Father and Sole Companion, Overseer of the Granaries, First Royal Herald, and Right Hand of the Lord of the Two Lands: Tell your brothers to bring their father and their families here as soon as they can. We will provide them with everything they need. Tell them not to worry if they have to leave some of their belongings behind, because the best of Egypt is theirs.

Joseph gave them wagons and abundant supplies and, for his father, forty donkeys loaded with grain, bread, and food for his journey. To each of the brothers he gave an elaborate ornamented robe and a goatskin pouch of silver. At first he was tempted to give Benjamin five of the splendid robes and triple the amount of silver, but when he contemplated the thought, he had to smile at its foolishness.

Still Alive

IT WAS EVENING WHEN THE BROTHERS arrived in Canaan. Zebulun leaped off his donkey and ran to Jacob's tent. "Father, Father!" he shouted. "Come outside. We have food for everyone, and wonderful news."

Jacob got up and walked out with him. The other ten sons were crowded around the tent's entrance.

"Joseph is still alive!" Simeon shouted, and there was a chorus of excited yeses.

"He's alive! We have seen him!" said Asher.

"Not only that," Judah said, taking Jacob's hand and gently stroking it, "but he is ruler over all Egypt."

"It's true, Father," Benjamin said.

Jacob stared at them as if they were madmen. What were they saying? It was impossible. How could the dead come back to life? Was this some kind of cruel joke? He remembered the other news, so many years before: the blood-soaked garment, the vision (it had never left him) of Joseph torn apart by a wild beast, that beautiful young body torn apart and devoured. How could that not be? Had it all been a dream? Was this a dream now, the story his sons were telling? Life becomes death; death doesn't become life. Or does it? When the seed is buried in the ground, it turns into a green stalk. Ah, but the metaphor is false. The seed hadn't been dead. It had just been dormant: life in a slower form.

Still, they said that Joseph was alive, that he was a great lord in Egypt, *the* great lord. Could it be true? They had recognized him; they had spoken to him. And all this magnificence—the ornamented robes, each as splendid as the coat he had once given to Joseph, the bags full of silver, the donkeys laden with grain—it had to come from *some*where, didn't it? He could see it and touch it. It, at least, was not a dream.

Trust them, the inner voice said. His heart eased. It might be true. It was too much to hope for, but it might be true.

My son Joseph may still be alive, he thought in dazed wonderment. *I will go see him before I die.*

The Secret

THE TEN BROTHERS COULDN'T BRING themselves to confess their crime. They had discussed it on the way to Canaan, on the second evening of their journey, exhaustively, fruitlessly, while Benjamin was asleep. None of them was able to face Jacob with the truth. They tried to imagine telling him, but it was too dreadful to contemplate.

Reuben said, "We could tell him that we just didn't know, that we found the coat and thought a wild beast had eaten Joseph."

"But Joseph will contradict that as soon as he talks with Father," Dan said.

"Yes," said Judah, "and a lie will only add to our guilt."

So they decided to say nothing.

Benjamin, the concubines, and the grandchildren came to their own conclusion: that Joseph had been attacked by a lion or wolf but had miraculously survived and made his way to Egypt. The story was believable, and there were no obvious inconsistencies. So it became the family's reality. Leah had her doubts, but she buried them under a rubble of evasions.

As for Jacob, it never occurred to him to question the story. Joseph had come back to life. That was all he cared about.

Nor, later on, did Joseph say anything to disabuse him. Jacob or Benjamin or one of the grandchildren might say, "When you were attacked by a wild beast . . . ," and Joseph would let it pass.

Occasionally, at first, he would catch a frightened look darting from one brother to another when someone made a comment like this, but the brothers quickly learned that their poor secret was safe with him.

To Goshen

THEY TOOK THEIR FATHER, LEAH, Bilhah, Zilpah, and their wives and children in the wagons that Pharaoh had sent them, and they traveled from Hebron to Goshen. The slaves were to follow, under the supervision of Issachar and Zebulun, bringing the flocks and herds with them.

Jacob was still in shock. He could feel a happiness dawning inside him, but it was as if he were watching it in a dream. Could he really dare to be happy? Leah sat beside him in the first wagon, holding his hand, encouraging him to trust what his sons had said. He knew, at least, that the threat of starvation was over. They were all fed now. The young grandchildren were bubbling with excitement at the adventure. Was he really on the way to Joseph? Would he be able to survive until they reached Egypt and not die of a bursting heart? Sometimes, as the wagon rattled along, he found himself talking to Rachel in his mind. *Joseph is alive, dearest. We are going to see him, you and I. We are going to bow down before him, all of us— sun, moon, and stars, just as he said we would.*

On the seventh day, Joseph rode out to meet them. When he saw his father, he leaped off his chariot and ran to him.

The old man looked like a fragment of his former self. He was terribly frail. Tears sprang to Joseph's eyes as he stood before him, and as he embraced him he began to sob—deep, body-wrenching sobs that rose from the well of joy, which is also the well of sorrow.

Jacob sobbed too. This was the unhoped-for consummation. He was seeing his beloved son. It was enough. It was far more than enough. Even if he were to live for another hundred years, the rest of his life would be just an afterthought, of unnecessary grace.

Compassion

AS THEY SETTLED INTO THEIR NEW LIVES in Goshen, Joseph could see that the ten brothers were still struggling under the burden of their guilt. They seemed fearful, or at least cautious, around him. It was obvious that they were living in the torturous world of the inner judge, whom they couldn't help imagining onto him, and also onto God. Because they weren't able to forgive themselves, they thought that he hadn't forgiven them, even though his words had presupposed it, even though his actions were filled with affection and largesse.

They had no idea who he was, and he didn't expect them to. They could perceive him only through eyes clouded with guilt and fear. In Joseph's world, they were all innocent, though guilty; in their world, they could have acted differently, and they had willfully chosen what was evil. In his world, he loved them; in their world, he despised them and was an expert dissembler, just waiting for their father to die before he inflicted some hideous punishment on them. Even Judah was trapped inside this overwhelming guilt. Joseph understood how painful it is to live in a mental world of good and evil, in which people consciously choose to think the thoughts that come into their minds and then consciously choose to believe those thoughts: a world in which God rewards and punishes people for actions that in reality they couldn't help, because those actions were the direct effects of those beliefs.

After two months, the brothers went to see Joseph in his palace, leaving Jacob and Benjamin in Goshen. The steward led them to the Great Hall. Joseph saw that they were troubled, and he cleared the room of Egyptians.

Judah was again their spokesman. "We beg you to forgive us for what we did to you so many years ago," he said. "We are truly sorry." All of them murmured their agreement and prostrated themselves before him.

It was as he had suspected. But this request for forgiveness, while it showed how little the brothers understood, was also a very good sign. It meant that the process of redemption was continuing. He would have to be very gentle with them. He would speak to them as if they were children.

"Don't be afraid," he said. "Am I God, who brings to pass everything that happens? Of *course* I forgive you. I forgave you a long time ago. Besides, although you wanted to harm me, God brought good out of it. He meant to save many lives, as we see today. So don't worry. I will continue to take care of you and your families, as I have up to now."

He was using the clearest language he could think of, but it was as if he were trying to draw a three-dimensional figure in two dimensions. That God had taken what is evil and turned it to good was something the brothers' minds would be able to grasp. But in reality, it wasn't like that. Their deed had been unkind and painful, yes, to them all, but it wasn't separable from the whole course of events, the complete pattern. When you isolated it, plucking it out of the flow of time, you falsified it. It had never existed by itself; it had never been a separate event apart from the dynamic whole. So how could you call it evil? In reality, God doesn't see anything as evil. Everything happens according to His will, on earth as in heaven. For God, it is all very good, as He said on the sixth day of Creation.* Joseph knew from long experience that the mind finds its proper balance in that sixth-day awareness. From it, the mind moves into its Sabbath, the peace that passes all understanding.

How could the brothers, in their present state of guilt, begin to comprehend the deep gratitude he felt for everything, even for those hours (or was it days?) he had spent in the pit, bruised and thirsty and foul with his own excrement, and frightened out of his mind, out of his precious identity? But it was that experience that had led to this fulfillment, and if even one step along the way had been eliminated or changed, the way would have led somewhere else, somewhere less.

There was nothing in it that he would change. There was nothing in it that he could call evil—not the pit, not the prison, not slander, famine, destruction, death. It had, all of it, led to this moment.

---

* Rabbi Eliezer bar Yehoshua of Megiddo said, "When you understand that God is within you, you cannot see anything as evil. As it is said, 'The Lord is in the midst of thee; thou shalt not see evil anymore.'" (Zeph. 3:15)

Epilogue

SO JOSEPH SETTLED HIS FATHER and brothers in Goshen, providing everything necessary for their comfort. He visited his father as often as he could, and he was generous and affectionate with his brothers, caring for their wives and children and helping them in every crisis. Slowly they began to trust him.

Joseph remained in the good graces of Pharaoh and his successor until the end of his life, and he continued to benefit the whole country with his compassionate wisdom. The years came and went. Jacob died. Joseph's sons had families of their own. The grandchildren became adults. Decades more went by. Joseph grew old, gracefully. He was able to continue working until the final two weeks of his life. Then his body began to shut down, and he took to his bed. He knew he was dying. Asenath knew it too.

All his adult life he had been living without a future, and it was no different now. His mind wasn't tempted to leap ahead of itself, into thoughts of what might or might not happen after the body died. Whatever state of existence or nonexistence followed, he trusted that it would be good. He didn't question the intelligence that had created everything in the universe and had led him with such astonishing kindness to this culminating moment.

He was fond of his body. It had been a faithful companion, never complaining, even when he had given it the most rigorous tasks and pushed it to its limits. It had always done its best, like a well-trained horse or a dog that adores its master. It had served him well, and now, when it needed to stop living, he had no quarrel with it.

Nor would he be sorry to leave his identity behind. He had enjoyed it, this collection of thoughts and passions that people had called "Joseph" or "Meri-Amun" or "Zaphnath-paneakh." More than enjoyed: he had great respect for it. It had known when to properly assert itself and when to step out of the way and give itself over to the unnamable. At those moments, there was not a trace of doing in it. It was a transparent vessel, an instrument, grateful to be used. But he was ready to leave this cherished identity behind now, along with the rest of his world, even his children, even his endlessly beloved Asenath. He had no regrets. There was nothing further he wished for, nothing he had left undone. Everything was coming to completion, like a long piece of music that has almost arrived at its final chord.

On the last day, he and Asenath gazed into each other's eyes. There was no fear or sorrow in them, only love.

◇

Notes and References

1 *the original Hebrew:* The "original" Hebrew? Hmm. The Masoretic text of the Joseph story, the one that has been handed down to us, is an edited version; any bright high-school senior can be taught how to recognize this. Most of it consists of the oldest layer, an unbroken unity without gaps. But into the story the editor of Genesis has inserted two long passages written centuries later and has spliced in many other scenes from various sources. For one reconstruction of a possible original, see my *Genesis: A New Translation of the Classic Biblical Stories* (New York: HarperCollins, 1996).

As for the "God" character, he does make an appearance in the Tamar story, just long enough to slay Er and Onan (Gen. 38:7–10), but this is not, strictly speaking, part of the Joseph story. There is also a brief, trivial appearance in the addenda to the story, at Gen. 46:2–4.

3 *seventy times seven:* Matt. 18:22.

3 *doesn't show us what forgiveness looks like:* In the parable of the Prodigal Son, the son hasn't committed any direct offenses against his father. (If I hurt myself, there's nothing for you to forgive.) It's true that the father welcomes him home with an open heart and accepts him unconditionally, but that's not the same thing as forgiveness. Nor, in the free-floating story that an editor spliced into the Gospel of John, has

the woman caught in adultery committed any offense against Jesus
that would call for his forgiveness.

3 *all hatred driven hence:* "A Prayer for my Daughter," in *The Collected
Works of W. B. Yeats,* vol. 1: *The Poems,* ed. Richard J. Finneran (New
York: Scribner, 1990), 189–90.

10 *entertained angels unawares:* Heb. 13:2.

18 *an old Zen poem:* "The Mind of Absolute Trust" by Seng-ts'an (?–606),
the Third Founding Teacher of Zen. See *The Enlightened Heart: An Anthology of Sacred Poetry,* ed. Stephen Mitchell (New York: Harper &
Row, 1989), 26–28.

23 *"A god has given us this leisure":* Virgil, *Eclogues* 1.6.

24 *Rabbi Meïr . . . Rabbi Shimon:* Genesis Rabbah 84:7.

26 *"The words of a talebearer":* Prov. 18:8.

29 *My worst fears have happened:* Job 3:25. *The Book of Job,* trans. Stephen
Mitchell (New York: Harper Perennial, 1992), 14.

48 *"The way up and the way down":* Heraclitus, fragment 60 (Diels-
Krantz).

48 *Instead of sleep, the remembered pain:* Aeschylus, *Agamemnon,* 179–83
(my translation).

67 *that is how our storyteller:* Actually, it was the editor who, with his keen
instinct for suspense, spliced the self-contained, independently circu-
lating "Judah and Tamar" into the Joseph story, where it fits brilliantly,
though with a few loose ends.

75 *the lovely priestesses: Gilgamesh: A New English Version,* trans. Stephen
Mitchell (New York: Free Press, 2004), 81.

86 *Rashi:* Acronym for Rabbi Shlomo Yitzhaki (1040–1105), French
commentator on the Bible and Talmud.

86 *"It is better to be cast into a fiery furnace":* Babylonian Talmud, Sot.
10b.

87 *When he makes a mistake: Tao Te Ching,* trans. Stephen Mitchell (New
York: Harper & Row, 1988), 61.

93 *a man loses half his soul: Odyssey,* 17.322–23:

> Zeus almighty takes half the good
out of a man on the day he becomes a slave.

(*The Odyssey,* trans. Stephen Mitchell [New York: Atria, 2013], 229.)

93 *content with the low places: Tao Te Ching*, trans. Stephen Mitchell, 8.

107 *"You shall love the Lord your God":* Deut. 6:5.

107 *that which, when discovered and attained:* In the famous first sentence of *On the Improvement of the Understanding*, Spinoza wrote, "After experience had taught me that all the ordinary events of life are vain and futile, since none of the objects of my fears contained anything that was either good or bad in itself, except insofar as the mind was affected by them, I finally decided to inquire whether there might be some real good that had the power to communicate itself and would affect the mind singly, to the exclusion of everything else: whether, in short, there might be anything that, when discovered and attained, would enable me to experience continuous, supreme, and never-ending joy." (My translation.)

108 *"The whole earth is full of His glory":* Isa. 6:3.

108 *an ancient Chinese Zen master:* Hsüeh-feng, 822–908 CE.

108 *"The scientist's religious feeling":* Albert Einstein, *Einstein sagt : Zitate, Einfälle, Gedanken*, ed. Alice Calaprice, München: Piper, 2005, 178. (My translation.)

108 *"Happy is the man":* Prov. 3:13.

113 *and then from legend:* That is, from the version in Genesis. More than two thousand years later, some medieval Arabic and Persian poets gave her the name Zuleika.

135 *The Maxims of Ptah-hotep:* Christian Jacq, *The Living Wisdom of Ancient Egypt* (New York: Pocket Books, 1999), 127, 76, 107 (translations modified).

149 *the still, small voice:* 1 Kings 19:12.

158 *"precious beyond all things":* Prov. 31:10.

162 *I have joined with my wife:* Gen. 2:24.

165 *"You appear on the horizon":* "Hymn to the Sun" by Pharaoh Amenhotep IV, a.k.a. Akhenaton (fourteenth century BCE), in *Bestiary: An Anthology of Poems about Animals*, ed. Stephen Mitchell (Berkeley, Calif.: Frog, Ltd., 1996), 3–4 (slightly revised). This hymn was the inspiration for the great Hebrew Psalm 104.

171 *Moshe ben Nachman:* 1194–1270. Known in Hebrew by the acronym Ramban and among Christians as Nachmanides.

171 *Fifth Commandment:* Exod. 20:12; Deut. 5:16.

176 *"You must not fool yourself":* Richard Feynman, California Institute of Technology commencement address, 1974.

189 *both in and out of the game:* Walt Whitman, "Song of Myself," in *Poetry and Prose* (New York: The Library of America, 1982), 30.

196 *"I have discovered . . . that all human misery":* Blaise Pascal, *Pensées,* Number 139 (Brunschvicg edition, 1914).

247 *the peace that passes all understanding:* Phil. 4:7.

Acknowledgments

My thanks to John Tarrant and Carol Williams, who made insightful suggestions about an early version of this book, and to Paul Auster, whose comments helped improve a late version.

Linda Loewenthal, my agent, opened my eyes to a new way of framing the story, gave the manuscript her meticulous attention, suggested unthought-of possibilities, and stretched me beyond my apparent limits. I am more grateful to her than I can say.

I am also deeply grateful to my editor, Joel Fotinos, for his enthusiastic support. Thanks are also due to the staff at St. Martin's Press, especially to Sona Vogel, my meticulous copyeditor.

Stephen Mitchell was born in Brooklyn in 1943, educated at Amherst, the Sorbonne, and Yale, and de-educated through intensive Zen training. His many books include the bestselling *Tao Te Ching, Gilgamesh, The Gospel According to Jesus, The Book of Job, The Second Book of the Tao, The Selected Poetry of Rainer Maria Rilke, Bhagavad Gita, The Iliad, The Odyssey,* and *Beowulf.* He is also the co-author of three of his wife Byron Katie's bestselling books.